STORIES OF RESILIENCE

Published by Northampton Borough Council Community Safety &
Engagement Team and University of Northampton Changemakers
Publishing partner: Paragon Publishing, Rothersthorpe

First published 2018

ISBN 978-1-78222-575-1

Book design, layout and production management by Into Print
www.intoprint.net
+44 (0)1604 832149

THIS COLLECTION OF short stories has been produced as a result of a partnership between Northampton Borough Council's Community Safety and Engagement team and the University of Northampton Changemakers.

These stories have been selected and collated in time to be launched and celebrated on International Women's Day 2018.

We would like to thank each member of the judging panel for contributing their time to help select and finalise this collection.
Most importantly, we would like to thank all of our inspirational authors for their submissions that made this project come to life.

Judges:

Victoria Boulton – *University of Northampton*
Sarah Passam – *Voluntary Impact Northamptonshire*
Elinor Cross – *BBC Radio Northampton*
Councillor Anna King – *Northampton Borough Council*

Contents

WEIGHT LOSS JOURNEY

Kerry

The start of 2015 I weighed 19 stone and had no confidence or self-esteem, was happily married (or so I thought). Being overweight resulted in me never wanting to go out to functions or parties etc. I would panic every time I received an invite. Worrying about what I would wear. I would try to find a suitable outfit, but a shopping trip always resulted in having to buy what fitted instead of what I liked, this would then make me dread the upcoming event even more. The negative thoughts I had about my weight and body sent me into a downward spiral of eating takeaways and not moving very much, which resulted in more weight piling on. It was vicious circle, one that I didn't think I would ever escape from. I felt safe within my four walls at home with hubby. As long as we were together, nothing else really mattered. However, I know he found it hard that I would shy away from events or gatherings, due to my lack of confidence, preferring instead to stay safe at home... of course with a takeaway or something to console myself with.

My hubby and I had never been lucky enough to have children and after several attempts at NHS procedures, I gave up the hope of ever being a mum. That was back in 2004ish. I could not face another month of hope and despair, so I gave up trying. And with that I gave up my dreams of having a family. At the time I was a little overweight, but not to the dizzy high figures of 19 stone, which is where I had reached in 2015. Coming to terms with never being a mother was so very hard and emotional. Looking back now I realise that I shut a lot of these emotions away within a box inside my head. Tried to carry on with life as though I was a tough cookie. I realise now, this was another reason my confidence started to nose dive. I was a failure and not normal. I wasn't like other normal women who married, fell pregnant and had babies. I was a freak! It turned out that hubby had fertility issues, however, I believed that as long as we had each other I could get through the future with just us two together. We would grow old together and look forward to other adventures that other couples with children couldn't do or afford. That's what I had hoped for anyway.

So back to 2015. Here I was. An overweight, middle aged lady with no confidence, gorging on takeaways for enjoyment. The morning that I decided that things needed to change was in February 2015. It was a Saturday morning, and hubby had gone off to play golf. I was driving to McDonalds to treat myself to a breakfast. An advert came on the radio, advertising a weight loss company where you could lose a stone a month if you followed their plan. In my head I made a promise to myself and a plan. I was going to do it! Finally shift the weight that had plagued me for so long and that was preventing me from truly living life. I made a 4-step plan for my 2015:

- *Save for a new kitchen*
- *Lose weight*
- *Go on a luxury holiday... hopefully the Maldives*
- *Get a new car*

A new kitchen had always been my dream... closely followed by the Maldives. However, I knew I would never go to the Maldives, carrying 19 stone in weight. A friend of mine had once followed a VLCD (very low calorie diet) plan with Lighterlife. I remember her losing her weight quickly and more importantly, she had kept it off! I had followed lots of diets in the past and always ended up putting the weight straight back on, and more! This time I was determined to make a change for good. I desperately wanted the new kitchen. I knew the diet plan wasn't cheap. I realised I couldn't save and do the diet at the same time. So, I planned to save every penny I had to purchase my dream kitchen, and then hopefully by the August I would have saved enough I could then start the diet. I told family and friends that come August I was doing the diet, which consisted of 4 replacement meals per day. I'm sure at the time they thought "oh yer, she will never do that!" After all, I was forever announcing I was starting a new diet "on Monday"… and Monday never came.

This time, however, I knew in my heart that it was different. I was excited (and nervous) to start the diet. I couldn't wait. I did lots of research and worked out how much per week it would cost me. I told hubby my plan. He didn't seem that excited about my 4-point plan. I put this down to him not believing I had the willpower to carry it out. I would prove him wrong!

He lost interest in a lot of things around the house. Not wanting to improve anything. He said it was work and that he wanted to find another job. I tried to help him with this, looking for job vacancies, updating his CV and encouraging him along the way. Nothing seemed to improve his mood.

Between February and August 2015, I saved and saved. By mid-July I started hunting around for kitchen quotes. After receiving a few quotes, I realised that my optimistic budget for a kitchen was way off of the mark and I would need to do a lot more saving before I could afford that. I was gutted but hubby didn't seem bothered at all. It felt like hard word trying to get him interested in discussing the new kitchen etc. I believed him when he said it was due to his work and felt sorry for him as his work was making him so unhappy.

End of July arrived and I finally was getting ready to start my diet. I said a last goodbye to all of my favourite treats. I drove to Milton Keynes to meet my new counsellor and have my first weigh in. I felt so ashamed standing on the scales and hearing how much I truly weighed. For the past couple of years I had avoided the scales completely. I obviously realised I was gaining weight but tried to bury my head in the sand and avoid accepting it. I would shop for new clothes and immediately cut the size label out of them. I was so ashamed. During my initial weigh in I had my photos taken. These would be my 'before' snaps. I told my counsellor I would like to lose 4 stone. (Initially thinking that that was all I needed to lose. HA!) She told me I would easily lose that by Xmas. In my head I didn't believe that possible.

So the 1st day arrived, I had a porridge for breakfast. A milkshake for lunch. A chocolate bar in the afternoon and a shepherd's pie for my tea. I was so chuffed with myself that I made it through my first day without cheating. YAY… I could do this. I was so excited for my next weigh in the following week. I completed my 1st week and didn't cheat once. I was proud of myself, which resulted in a 6lb loss. I knew that this was the diet for me! I felt great and had so much more energy.

After week 3 I had lost a stone. A whole stone… gone forever! … That was before the bombshell that awaited me when I arrived home from work one day.

11

I came through the door. Said 'Hello' to hubby and asked if he was ok. To which he replied he wasn't ... *eeek* I thought. What's happened? The look on his face told me it looked like bad news. He then proceeded to tell me that he was no longer happy at home with me. We had been together for 23 years. My world fell apart at that moment. Time stood still. My future was no longer what I had imagined it would be. I listened to him tell me why he was unhappy. I told him that I knew there was someone else, which he denied, although in my heart I knew there was. He then walked out. At that moment I was in shock. Didn't know what to say or do. My immediate reaction was to open the fridge. I thought to myself, why bother trying to lose weight and better myself. There really was no point anymore. I picked up a block of cheese. I may as well give up. I was looking for comfort. Trying to hide from the world again! At that moment, I decided not to give in. If there was any time that I needed to do something for myself and make a better life for me ... it was right now. Right in this moment! I was at a crossroads and I was determined not to go down the dark path of more weight gain and unhappiness. I had to be strong! So I put down the cheese and shut the fridge and would try to deal with this emotional crisis without the comfort of food.

Apart from immediate family, I didn't tell anyone about my world falling apart. This was mainly because I couldn't face what was happening. How could I explain to anyone what had happened and why, when I couldn't explain it to myself or to come to terms with it? My now ex and I remained amicable with each other. Mainly because I did not want the stress of arguments or anger, but believe me, I felt it inside. Again, I bottled things up. I then started to hear the rumours swirling around the village that he had been seeing someone for months, since early that year. Every rumour or truth I heard was like another dagger in my heart. I then uncovered text messages and discovered that he was texting this 'person' (sorry but I can't bring myself to call her a lady) ... Up to 3000 times a month! That equated to almost 70 texts per day! *Every* day! But still he insisted that there was no one else involved. I believed in my heart this was untrue. Again, I didn't confront him with the texts or rumours I had heard. What was the point? I had asked myself. I would never get the truth. I believe that he was trying to protect me from it, to prevent hurting me more than he had to. Instead I had to build up a picture / story of what had gone on. I relived the last few months... looking for clues and putting pieces of the puzzle together. In some cases coming up with the wrong picture, but in others, I know the puzzle was complete.

So, what of the diet! I pushed onwards with it and the weight continued to fall off. By December 2015 I was a size 16. Down from a size 24/26 at the start of the diet. Although on the outside I was rebuilding myself, inside I was a broken woman with a future of nothing ahead of me. No one to share it with. I was having legal appointments to sort out the financial side of the split. Doing things I never ever dreamed I would have to do... and having to do it alone! Going through that process alone certainly made me stronger and more independent.

By April 2016, I had reached my target weight and had lost 9½ stone. That was a loss of a stone per month! I now weighed 9 stone 5 lbs. Physically I felt great, until that is, I found a breast lump. Seriously! What more could go wrong? After a couple of weeks of worry, it turned out to be benign. Thankfully!

I needed a holiday. I booked a week away with my mum to Greece. A short break in the sunshine, before having the operation to have the lump removed. Whilst in Greece I wore a bikini for the 1st time in ages. It felt great to feel what is socially accepted as 'normal'. During that holiday I had a medical emergency. I fainted one morning in the bathroom. I put it down to getting up too quickly. However, later that day, I developed immense abdominal pains. I was doubled over in pain and had to call the emergency doctor out. After examining me, he said he felt something he didn't like the feel of. But he didn't give me any more information. The language was quite a barrier. He gave me a couple of injections and told me to seek advice from my GP upon my return home.

Once home, I was diagnosed with gallstones and needed to have my gallbladder removed. I was booked in for the 'routine' keyhole operation which I was told would be day surgery. I don't remember a great deal of what happened next. I fuzzily remember coming around after the operation in recovery and remember a nurse checking my blood pressure etc. She said that she was worried as my blood pressure was dropping … I was so thirsty, I told her it was probably just because I needed a cup of tea. Lol. How wrong was I?!

I sort of remember them calling my parents to tell them that I needed another emergency operation so they could open me up and see what was going on as my stats were dropping very low. The next thing I remember was waking up on the High Dependency ward after a 2nd operation where they had had to cut me open and they then found that during the 1st operation they had cut my umbilical artery when they were removing the camera. I had had an internal haemorrhage and had to have a blood transfusion to replace the 3 pints of blood that I had lost. I was fitted with a catheter and I was in a great deal of pain. At that moment I just wanted someone close to give me a big hug. I felt so very very low and alone. I remember my parents coming to visit me and me bursting into tears when they said they would go home. I desperately didn't want to me alone. Everything that had happened the previous 9 months hit me like a ton of bricks. Hearing your doctor say the words *"you could have died following the haemorrhage"* and I'm sure the drugs I was being pumped with along with the anaesthetic, played a part in the way I was feeling.

It took me a long time to recover from this operation. My blood pressure and liver took such a long time to get back to a normal state. I'm still suffering the after effects even now. I now know there is no such thing as a routine operation.

∾

So two years down the line from when I started my diet and hubby left me … I'm still standing! I'm maintaining my weight loss. I will *NEVER* go back to the weight I was. I'm not obsessed with the scales. I'm just conscious of what I eat. I still have my treat days, but also have my strict days. My day to day diet is a balance of treats and healthy foods. This is a balance I never discovered before the start of my diet journey.

My confidence is slowly coming back, although this is taking longer than I thought it would. It's hard to readjust to the image I now see in the mirror before me. I still feel like the fat girl driving to McDonalds for that breakfast treat back at the start of 2015.

The past few years have been so emotional, stressful and testing for me. My family have been amazing. My parents have been a tower of strength to me and I know I would not have made it to where I am now, had they not been there with me every step of the way, giving me love and support.

As I predicted the day he told me he was unhappy and that our marriage was over, ex hubby has moved in with the person whom he was texting 70 times every day. My divorce has just been finalised so I now have to move on with my life ... and hopefully find a life partner to share it with me.

A stronger, slimmer and more independent me!

I'm ready!

LIFE CHANGE

Aftermath

Twelve years ago, I had it all, partner, two beautiful daughters and a career in teaching Art. Then, ten years ago. My relationship broke down, my daughters and myself moved out to a smaller house and for a while things were hard but ok.

Then one day I was invited to come to a barbeque by the parents of one of my eldest daughter's friends. We had a lovely afternoon and then we started playing badminton in their garden. I was game so I took a racket and had a good time until I reached too far and too high and crashed down backwards onto a basket with wood logs, a concrete slabbed floor, narrowly avoiding a motorbike that was parked there as well. I hurt my back and shortly after took a taxi home.

The pain in my back wouldn't go away and although this happened in 1996 it wasn't until 1999 that an MRI scan revealed that I had *Multi-Level Degenerative Disc Disease*, a whole row of slipped and damaged discs in my spine. I began taking painkillers and having the odd extra glass of wine to ease the pain and help me sleep. Little did I know this was the start of a ten-year struggle which I'm only just coming to terms with now?

By that time, I was Deputy Head of a School in Northampton for children with serious behavioural difficulties, financially independent and although I walked with crutches I was happy and content. Then the school where I worked rescheduled their management system and offered me a different job I couldn't take because of the risk of my back being damaged further, and me ending up in a wheelchair, so I retired on Medical Grounds and entered the benefit system.

This is when it all began and with it my consumption of wine grew slowly but steadily. I applied for DLA and was refused so I took counsel at Community Law Services and appealed their decision. I ended up going to a Tribunal, on my own, which had a successful outcome: they overruled the original decision. Being in receipt of DLA meant I could start looking at having a Motability car, which I started looking into.

In the meantime my pains hadn't gone away but in fact gotten worse so I was referred to a Rheumatologist who diagnosed me with Inflammatory (Psoriatic) Arthritis and a year later with Fibromyalgia as well. I became depressed, was on 300 tablets plus a week and felt ill from them all the time. I also slept a lot, helped by a generous intake of red wine. This became too much and I was visited by two nurses from my

GP practice who advised me to undergo a home detox and helped me organise my tablets in a blister-pack that was delivered once a week.

So here I was: three disabilities, Depression and IBS, continuous pain in my spine, my joints and all the soft tissue; and no hope for improvement. I started the detox and did well for a number of years by abstaining from alcohol; and just dealing with the pain of my conditions. I felt like I lost it all; no relationship, no job, no financial independence, restricted movement, and constant relentless pain whether I moved or not. But I was off the booze and that felt good.

With the help of a practitioner at Aquarius I dealt with issues that came my way and received some support in my situation. We even worked out together what type of car I would go for from the Motability range. I went through a few years of calm before the storm: someone offered me a drink and I thought I had overcome my drink problem and could easily do this and not worry about anything. How wrong I was!

That one glass, in my eyes, meant I could cope with alcohol so I started to drink wine again, moderately at first but after re-finding out how much better it made me feel and sleep it became a habit and then a full-blown dependency. Still, I would have denied that I was an alcoholic. But the problems it caused were many, I was offered an all-expenses paid for trip to visit my family and friends abroad but I couldn't go, I was too weak from the alcohol, felt too ashamed and simply left my packed suitcase standing waiting in my bedroom while I continued mixing my medication with alcohol with all the consequences thereof. I became ill and more ill, suffered from vomiting and diarrhoea and in my home things weren't well either. My eldest daughter had left for University but my youngest daughter suffered being a young carer of a triple invalid and an alcoholic mother to boot.

I was warned that should I need an ambulance again to take me to the hospital because of my drinking that Social Services would become involved and so they were: my youngest left me to go and live with her father while I sorted myself out. I denied it all for a while and kept on drinking until even I understood that I should make changes if I ever wanted a normal live and a normal relationship with my daughters. I was weak, ill, drunk most of the time, had almost no contact left with friends and finally admitted to my practitioner friend from Aquarius that I had suffered a relapse and that I needed to sort many things out in order to get my life back on track.

We started looking at making an application for supported housing from the Council and without his help nothing would have happened on time: I was simply not organised and strong enough to deal with it all. I decided to go for another detox and asked my GP for help. They agreed to assist me with a home detox and a finished the last of my wine with a determined feeling that this was it now, I was going to beat this thing called alcohol dependency or alcoholism, whatever term you want to use, and I did.

For nearly nine months now I have been sober and have not touched a drop. I have had ongoing support from Aquarius and my ex-partner who was there when I needed him. My medication works as it should especially after I stopped taking one pill that made me sleep a lot. I've been to visit my friends and family abroad successfully, organised a lot for and celebrated Christmas with both my daughters, grandson and ex-partner. I have been accepted on the Council Housing List and can bid on properties that suit my disabilities better then where I now live. I've picked up online courses I ordered a few years ago and am now working through them and the future looks good.

I can only speak from my own experience but I would say to anyone who gets faced with difficult situations, don't give up, go for and accept help and don't worry if it takes time to get things right: Rome wasn't built in a day. I still dream about wine and wake up scared that I started drinking again, then soon realise that I'm done with that. I look towards the future now with hope and a sense of self-worth and confidence which I didn't have while I was drinking and struggling to come to term with three disabilities and Depression and IBS. And let no one tell you it cannot be done: I've been there and done it, and if I can do it so can you! I wish you all the strength and love you need.

24

ENDOMETRIOSIS

Carrie

Hello, my name is Carrie and I am currently 21 years old. I was diagnosed with Endometriosis on the 4th April 2016 via an experimental Laparoscopy at a local private hospital. The Endometriosis was removed during this procedure and when I came around from the anaesthetic I was given my diagnosis. However, my story does not start there.

I started my periods at the age of 12 and have always had bad experiences with them. I often had time off of school or went to school with a hot water bottle due to excessive pain when menstruating. At the age of 14 I had already had enough of the pain I was enduring each month and I went to the doctors where I was put on a non-contraceptive pill, which I had to take three times a day to stop me having periods. At the age of 16 I was put onto a contraceptive pill, again one to stop me having periods. After still having pain in my abdomen I went back to the doctors and had the implant.

This worked for a year. During this time I often had pain during sexual intercourse, and sometimes even bleeding. After a year I had a four month long period. I went back to the doctors and this is when I was referred to a specialist gynaecologist at the age of 17. At this consultation Endometriosis was not mentioned at all. I was given the Mirena coil and told that this should stop the pain and the bleeding. I was discharged from this consultant after which I went back to the doctors due to chronic lower back pain. The doctor I saw was so helpful. She explained to me that the pain I was feeling in my lower back was due to how tense the muscles in my lower abdomen were, she once again referred me to a specialist gynaecologist. This takes me to where I was seen and had my Laparoscopy at the age of 20 – eight years after starting to suffer with the chronic pain of Endometriosis.

After my Laparoscopy I was given a check-up appointment six months later. I had a wonderful, pain free month after my Laparoscopy before the pain started again.

At first it was bearable and I could cope with just taking regular pain medication and managed to get on with my life relatively well. I managed to live life like a normal 21 year old should be able to do. In August 2016 I collapsed on a night out for my best friend's birthday. The bouncer's son of the club we were in luckily recognised me and my friends and he drove us to the A&E department. I was admitted to hospital for five nights. During these five nights I was pumped with: Morphine, Codeine and many other types of painkillers to try and keep the pain at bay. I was discharged home with a promise I would have an appointment with the gynaecologist that carried out my Laparoscopy within a week.

A month after being discharged I was re-admitted to hospital for one night due to the pain being excessive and me not being able to cope on the painkillers I had at home. It was three months before I had an appointment with the gynaecologist.

At this appointment I was told that my Endometriosis was not back and the pain I was feeling was all in my head. I was told that I would need to have psychological help in the form of a therapy called Cognitive Behavioural Therapy. As a student Mental Health nurse, I knew that this therapy entailed different exercises to change the way you think. I knew that the pain was real and therapy would not help me. I often spent time sat down A&E in excruciating pain hoping to be given just some sort of release – this pain I could *not* make up in my head.

The gynaecologist agreed to send me to the pain management clinic. At this point I was fed up and desperate for help and answers. At the pain management appointment I was listened to and understood, the doctor I saw there was lovely. She agreed with me that Cognitive Behavioural Therapy would not help me so she referred me to the John Radcliffe hospital in Oxford.

At my first appointment in Oxford I was seen for an hour by a specialist gynaecologist who went through my whole eight years of pain, appointments and anything that seemed to be relevant to the pain I was feeling. At this appointment I was referred to: a physiotherapist to help with how tense my abdomen muscles have become, a psychologist to help me with the stress of suffering with Endometriosis and for an MRI scan to see whether or not the Endometriosis had returned.

I had my MRI scan in May 2017, a year after my first Laparoscopy. The Endometriosis had not only come back but it had spread. At first it was just attacking the outside of my womb. I now have Endometriosis on: my right ovary, the outside of my womb, my bowel and the gap between the bowel and the womb. This brings us to now. I am awaiting surgery at Oxford to remove the Endometriosis again. However, because this time it is a *'complex case'*, as the gynaecologist has referred to it, a meeting needs to be held with different doctors and surgeons to see who will carry out the surgery.

The pain is getting increasingly worse. I have had to take weeks off university and work due to the pain. I spend a lot of time at appointments and in A&E due to the pain. I have to take a cocktail of painkillers on a daily basis just to allow me to get out of bed. My family and fiancé fear when I go anywhere far away from them just in case I am admitted to hospital again. I fear to go out and enjoy myself in case the pain gets too much. I am scared to be a normal 21 year old again. However, the hope that the surgery will be soon keeps me going and I have incredible support from my fiancé, family and friends. They are all very understanding and will do anything to help me be out of this pain. Without them, the experience of Endometriosis would have been a lot worse. I hope one day to have children. I also hope that one day I will say I am Endometriosis free!

Danny

Hi, my name is Danny, I am 25 years old (even though I don't act like it). Before I started the Prince's Trust I wasn't doing anything, I was unemployed and looking for a job but unfortunately I didn't have any luck. I decided to go on the course because I wanted to get help finding a job as a receptionist. I also wanted to build up my confidence as I was not very confident. I also wanted to meet some new friends and make some new memories. And that I have done.

Thanks to the Prince's Trust I have now gained so much more confidence in myself. I have also made some amazing friends who hopefully I will stay in contact with after the course has finished. And I have also now got a qualification which I can use on my CV to increase my chances of finding my job as a receptionist.

I have enjoyed every bit of the course, including meeting all the team and making some amazing friends. My most memorable time was on the residential when we were all having a laugh and then Libby started chasing Emma and me around the bedroom with a toothbrush. We were all in stitches for the whole night crying with laughter, and this is one of the reasons why I'm so glad that I have come to this course as I have made memories like these.

After the Prince's Trust has finished I am going to carry on my search for a job as a receptionist or a care worker. Even though I didn't receive a job with the Prince's Trust my confidence has boosted up so much more than I had imagined it would.

Finally, I would like to say my thank-yous.

Firstly, thank you to Siobhan and Ryan because you have opened my eyes to different things within the job side of things.

Secondly, I would like to say thanks to Emma, Libby and Amy for being good friends and supporting me thoughout the 12 weeks.

Libby for helping me build my confidence up even more with introducing me to new people at the studio and helping me sing on stage and helping me through the residential when I found it hard in the cave and the night walk as I don't like the dark and I didn't know where we were going and we were in a small space.

Emma and Amy for being there on the walk which I really hated as I couldn't do all 7 miles but I did make it to 3.5 miles, and for making me laugh my head off. Emma has made my 12 weeks more enjoyable as we clicked from the first day. She has kept me going and helped me to attend the course getting me up in the morning.

And even though I didn't really talk to Amy at first during these 12 weeks we have bonded and now we are best friends. I hope that we won't lose our friendship with everyone.

CONFIDENCE BOOST

Emma

Hi, my name is Emma and I am 18 years old. Since I was born I was always involved with social services as I didn't have a great upbringing. I lived in a house where there was a lot of violence and mental health problems. At the age of 8 my granddad passed away and I was broken as he was my hero, I always loved going to see him even though I only saw him twice a year, however it all brightened up when my little brother was born. He made me so happy and I swore always to be the best big sister ever. I had to look after him as well as my mum so I became a young carer, because my dad worked all day and didn't get home till late.

I often missed a lot of school to look after my brother as my mum couldn't as she had mental health issues. I would cook and clean and make sure my brother was looked after. A year later my other little brother was born. He had to have an operation as he couldn't breathe properly and we thought that we were going to lose him as we were told he wasn't going to make it. But gladly he *did* make it and we spent Christmas as a family.

However, because of the violence I had to leave the house and stay with my neighbour in *kindership care*. I stayed there for a year and always saw my parents and my brothers. When I moved back home the violence got worse and police had to get called out on separate occasions. I had many sleepless nights and things became worse.

On my brother's 3rd birthday myself and my two brothers got put into care.

The next two years were the hardest I went through as there were courts for my brothers to go back to my parents, however they didn't want *me* back. I still saw my brothers every two weeks, which was okay. However, now they are adopted so I only see them twice a year which is very, very difficult as they are my world but I know that they are happy.

I stayed in care moving around Northamptonshire four times trying to find the right family. This made my anxiety worse as I felt unwanted and that I was being passed around. However, three years later I found my foster family which I lived with for a year, and I still keep in contact.

During all of this I was also in a mentally abusive relationship, I thought I had found the right person, however, he took me away from my family friends, made me lie to them so I couldn't be trusted. After two years of being in this relationship I finally escaped it.

However, it made me go really downhill and I was diagnosed with severe anxiety and depression.

I moved into my own flat and I had a really supportive boyfriend who I'm still with today who has helped me battle through my depression and my past.

Before I came to the Princes Trust I did my Level 2 in Childcare. My first job wasn't great as I got bullied, so I moved to a better job. After completing my Level 2 I started my Level 3 but found that it wasn't what I thought it was, so I left my job and ended up just staying at home by myself becoming more depressed. Then one day my PA told me about the Prince's Trust and truthfully I didn't want to go as I was very nervous and my anxiety was at its peak. However, I came to the Prince's Trust as I didn't want to just stay in bed thinking about my life and feeling bad about myself, because I wanted a job and a future and yes, to be truthful, also to stop everyone asking me to go!

I'm so glad that I came though as I have made some amazing friends which I can't thank enough. I have also made some amazing memories during the 12 weeks which I won't forget. My confidence has grown so much and my anxiety and depression has calmed down so much as before this course I wouldn't even *dream* of standing on a stage in front of a lot of people – during the final presentation we had to.

I enjoyed every moment of the 12 weeks, from every laugh to every upset as they have all made us strong and great friends. All my memories are just of all of us laughing constantly, cheering each other up. I remember on residential when me, Danny and another girl, who isn't on the course any longer, were up until late at night laughing our heads off at funny immature words (which I can't repeat) but I have never laughed so much at.

Thanks to the course I have found my future career as I have found a job in a care home, which I never thought I would want to work in until I did my work experience, and I have now found what I want to do.

Last but not least I want to say my thanks, firstly to my PA for getting me to the course in the first place because without her I wouldn't have all the friends and memories that I have. I also want to thank all the leaders and volunteers as they have helped me boost my confidence and helped me get a path in life and I can't thank them enough. I also want to thank my team members as they have helped me overcome my fears and boost my confidence, they have made me gain great memories and I've had some great laughs with all of them – even with our ups and downs.

Lastly, I have one more thanks – and this is going to make her cry – but I want to thank Danny. She has been the most amazing friend on this course. I remember the first day when I wouldn't talk to anyone and we got paired together and yeah at first it was awkward but we had a great laugh together from day one. She has supported me all through the course helping me with my anxiety through residential and standing up here today. She's constantly looking out for me, making sure that I'm OK, and without her being on the course with me I wouldn't have half the memories and the confidence I have now. So thank you *so* much for being there and helping me and being such an amazing friend.

WINNING THE BATTLE

Libby

My name is Libby. I am a nineteen year old and I live on my own in Northampton. Life has never been easy for me, the saying *fight through your battles* was not an option for me either, but a life style – it was either fight and be happy, or sit around and let life shut me down. I grew up with drugs and abusive parents that were too involved in their own lives. It turned into abandonment, this then caused me to be in and out of hospital from a week old. After two years of struggle my little brother came along, but it was like they never noticed him either. I mothered him from the day he was born, even though I was just a toddler myself. In the end they gave up on me and put me and my brother up for adoption. I am one of many children that didn't manage to escape from the harsh reality that is life, but I was helped. This did not mean that life was easy.

When I was five I was told I found a *forever family*. In my head it was all happy – finally someone loved me and wanted my brother to come with me and that was ideal. Turned out this incredible thing wasn't so delightful. At the age of nine they gave up on me … and kept my brother.

The issues varied. From many I could understand that these people – my supposed *forever family* – weren't my real mom and dad. I didn't have parents like the other children which excluded me from everyone else. Why did all the other kids have moms and dads? My brother was too young to understand, he thought this forever family were his real parents. He could accept these people as Mom and Dad as I couldn't. This made me angry, made me resent them and this turned me into an angry child. I couldn't accept the fact I was so different to everyone else. I hurt anyone I knew that tried to involve themselves in my life.

Eventually, after 12 years, 20+ homes, 19 social workers and 4 schools, I found an incredible woman named Jane. Without Jane I wouldn't be where I am now. She said to me: *"Look Libby, you have had a really bad 12 years, do you really want the rest of your life to be so unsettled?"*

Who knew the day I moved in my life was to change for the better. I didn't believe this. Why would I? Life did nothing but shut me down. 22nd January 2010 was what I would class as the best day of my life – someone *cared*.

When you are in care you are always fighting with the battles that 'I will never have the life others take for granted'. I settled, I learnt that this wasn't going to change, I had to accept the good that Jane gave me and take the opportunities that I was given, that I was never given before.

I lived with Jane for just about seven years. I will never forget what this woman did for me. On December 21st 2015 I got a call from the police asking to talk to my foster carer Jane. Jane didn't know what was up so I put it on speaker. This is where I found out my foster sister, Jane's real daughter, died in a car accident the night before. I was out driving and had to drive home to meet the police in order to give us information on how to proceed. Vicky died of head, neck and chest injuries as a passenger in the car with her boyfriend. No drink or drugs were involved, just a happy couple coming home from a meal out and all we know is they went into the back of a lorry. They both where killed outright.

I noticed that this incredible person Jane was never going to be the same, she hurt too much. The struggles of losing someone then began. Not only was the funeral complicated and took forever to prepare for, she realised the person she brought into her life was another version of her precious daughter. That version being me. Everything I did, said, spoke and did was exactly like Vicky. This understandably was hard for Jane to watch, she just kept seeing Vicky in me. I don't resent Jane for what I am about to tell you. Jane said to me: *"Libby I can't do this, I need you to leave."* This was followed with arguments and in the end I left. The anger hurt, took over me and I hated her at the time – it was yet another person that had let me down.

I ended up being homeless, living when and where I could, I didn't care. As far as I was concerned I lost my barrier that made everything OK. I ended up moving into Wellingborough and I lived there for a painful eight months. This meant I lost my place at college, a lot of friends and everything I loved – my horse riding, my scouting and singing group – it took forever to find a comfort zone and to accept I was on my own again. Now I live on my own in St James, I stay in contact with my brother when and where I can.

When I moved it was time I built something new again. I wanted work in order to pay for a uni course. For a while this was hard to accept. When I was looking for work I did some education and living courses to keep me occupied. Two people that have help me massively while living in St James are Grace and Abbie. Now, without big heads you guys you're incredible. Together you both make me smile and reassure me when I do right from wrong – this is very confidence giving.

Abbie, without you I would have been a mess when I moved in, as I'm not someone that is easily persuaded to do anything. I will do want I want to do *when* I want to do it, but despite my stubbornness you have a way about you that allows you to do what I need to do my way while knowing I'm doing right.

You are very patient and you have to be to have me, and to think when you had me you were told I'd be an easy one…

Grace. Oh Grace, what can I say for you? The one thing that made me like you so much is yet again your patience and your willingness to let me rant when I need and as I am sure you know I can ramble on when I need to but no matter what, you are there for me.

I joined the Prince's Trust as something to do while looking for a job and to help with job skills. I have not only gained a qualification through this, but new friends, catching up with old ones and some great opportunities that I probably won't get again. For example, I am the one person that can go weaseling and get stuck in a hole! I did amuse Grace though when I said I popped my head out like a badger but the rest wasn't going to budge. I ended up having to do the whole tunnel backwards, not being able to see where I was going. I eventually got out then almost cried when the instructor said to me, *"Oh, you should 've taken off a few layers then you would have been fine."*

The best week for me was definitely residential. This was more than team building, we got to understand one another and that was an incredible opportunity.

I want to thank Siobhan, Ryan, Shannon, Georgia and James for helping make our time unforgettable – and for someone that was so unwilling to do the course to begin with, I will *never* forget or regret doing it.

MY BROTHER'S SUICIDE

Anna Lou

Did my brother commit suicide because he felt he couldn't ask for help?

It was World Mental Health Day on October 10. A year to the day that I got the phone call to tell me my brother had committed suicide.

A year since I went from having a brother called Chrissy, to being someone who used to have a brother called Chrissy.

It was 12.50pm on a Friday when I got the call:

"Lou, it's your brother. I'm so sorry love, but he's gone, he's died."

I have two brothers, and the youngest had recently been in hospital with a DVT. How could he have died, he was taking blood thinning tablets, he'd looked pretty healthy the last time I saw him…?

As if hearing my thoughts, the voice at the other end of the phone clarified.

"It's not Karl…it's Chris, it's awful Lou, I'm sorry, he's hung himself."

In that moment, everything stopped and crystallized like I'd just put on a pair of super-charged glasses. Like I was viewing the world in high definition. The inside of my head buzzed and fizzed like I was about to short circuit.

I distinctly remember the solitary chime of the clock that rang out in Soho Square, and thinking the last time I'd heard the chime, he was still breathing. Still like me.

Chris was gone. The brother who was born in the same year as me, but wasn't my twin. Irish twins it's called. Born 11 months apart, stuck at the hip while we were kids, the one who used to take the flak for all my mischief.

In the after-shock, I felt like my arms and legs were riddled with pins and needles while my brain bounced around my skull like a pinball. It had only been a matter of hours since he'd died. I convinced myself that he could be kick-started back to life, like with a big iPhone charger for people. Surely there'd still be enough energy left just to give him a few percent…

~

In the days and weeks that followed, there wasn't much room in my head for very much more than him.

Death is devastating on all levels, but suicide brings with it an element of participation. Why hadn't I done anything to stop it? Why hadn't he spoken to me?

Just why?

We'll never know if Chris was mentally ill, depressed, or whether he just decided in that split second that enough was enough. But we do know that suicide is the biggest killer of men between 20 and 49, beating road accidents, cancer and coronary heart disease. I knew suicide in men was a problem, even before my brother plumped for it. In fact a couple of weeks before he died, I posted something on my Facebook page, urging people to be aware of the men in their lives: teenage student boys who might be struggling; unemployed Dads who might be feeling the pressure but bottling it all up inside.

But how aware was I of his despair?

Looking back, I knew something wasn't quite right. The softness had gone from him. Any sense of calmness had long since departed and he was a big angry ball of rage and frustration. I think he was angry at himself, but he could never admit that.

"It's not me," he'd shout, *"it's everyone else."*

But maybe that was his cry for help, because he didn't know how to say it any other way, or didn't feel that he could.

None of us really know the true face of depression or mental illness, or what mask each of us wears. It can be someone simply grasping for an even base line, but feeling like they're trying to nail jelly to the wall, or it can be someone who looks like sunshine, because they're radiating all the light out, and getting dimmer inside. It can be a big ball of anger, or a small pool of tears; it can be all of us. It's hard for people to reach out, but it's even harder for men.

When a person commits suicide they are often so distressed and isolated, they are unable to see any other way out. They often give warning signs in the hope that they will be rescued, because they are intent on stopping their emotional pain, not necessarily on dying. And looking back, the signs were there. I had them in texts on my phone, in the memories of our last time together. Finger-pointing, blame and frustration. Threats, which I thought were empty. I'd tried to talk to him, but he either felt like I wouldn't listen or he just couldn't say what he needed to say.

One of the last texts I sent to him pleaded with him to stop being so angry and closed off.

"Chris, I've posted something on Facebook about people who get in bad situations and things just spiral out of control. You have three gorgeous kids, a beautiful granddaughter and you have YOU. You don't have to give up on yourself. You can get everything back on track. Stop being so angry at everyone. I love you and

want my brother back. Please find some strength to get yourself back on track. This should be the beginning, not the end. If life begins at 40, grab it by the balls."

He didn't make 40, he was two months short of that milestone and I couldn't help him.

It's too late for Chrissy, but it's not too late for other men stood on the precipice of a black hole just waiting to jump. Whether he was mentally ill, depressed or feeling overwhelmed, the fact was he didn't feel like he could tell anyone. Like a lot of men, he would have seen reaching out as a dent on his masculinity, and as long as society perpetuates this cycle, more men will see suicide as the only option.

We all need to stand together and show that asking for help isn't weak. It isn't shameful. We need to help reduce the stigma around depression, mental health and suicide, and reach out to the men who are suffering in agonizing silence.

In a bid to make even the smallest difference, I recently started working for a mental health charity. It's just baby steps, possibly only making a tiny indent into what is a massive problem, but I'm hoping to make what difference I can (knowing that it was you Chris, who helped make the difference to me).

UNITED WOMEN

Emma

Resilience is something that has come and gone throughout my whole life. It wasn't until I sat down to write this, that I realised how resilient at times I have needed to be. The earliest memory of when resilience became part of my life, was when I was six years old. My family and I were on holiday in South Africa visiting my grandparents and cousins, when three children came running up to the car window. Clearly struggling to support themselves, one child around my age asked us to buy their wonderfully crafted clay animal souvenirs. This moment in my life as a six-year-old sparked my compassion for charity work, and from then my passion to help others started to bloom.

The next time my passion became apparent, was in secondary school. My father came back from my parents evening, and reported back what the deputy head had said about me. He had commented that in the past two months, I had knocked on his door multiple times asking if we could do fundraising and awareness raising for different charities and that I wouldn't let him get away with not doing an event. I felt that my experience in South Africa spurred me on to try and make a difference, even if it was small. Sivananda Saraswati said that "oceans are made up of tiny droplets", and this resounds clearly with my initial passion for charity work.

I felt that even though we were doing fundraising events for large charities such as Oxfam and Worldvision, I wanted to be more hands-on, and meet the people the charities were helping. So, a week before Christmas when I was 15 years old I asked my father if we could go and help at the local homeless shelter in Cardiff, where I was living. My father, being supportive of my passion, rang the local homeless shelter and asked if we could come and volunteer at the shelter. Much to my disappointment, volunteers had to be at least 18 years old. However, this did not stop me. It showed that resilience is vital, if you want to follow your passion and stand up for what you believe in.

Finally, I turned 17 years old, and was almost an adult, building on my desire to follow my passions and make my own decisions. It's an important time in one's life when you're 17, and doing your A-levels. You are expected to sit down and decide what you want to do with the rest of your life. Schools always strive to help you with this big decision that will depict the rest of your life. Which university will you attend? What are you going to study at university? What grades do you need to get into university? So off I went to a universities fair to help me decide the answers to all these looming questions. The fair is where I found the answer to the next step in my life. Instead of selecting the best university and degree course, I ended up talking to someone about volunteering as a primary school teacher in Malawi for a year. From then, my life changed.

It provided the insight and an opportunity for my passion to help people to become reality. One problem though, how was I going to tell my parents? With my brother studying dentistry at Cardiff University, I felt that I was expected to follow in his footsteps, and achieve, by doing something great with my life. I called a family meeting. Only something done in emergencies within our family. My mother sat me down, concerned, just before my father arrived for the meeting, and asked me if I was going to tell them something dreadful, and to tell her prior to my father's arrival, to enable us to resolve the problem together. I just laughed, and said, "Mum, don't worry it's not bad news, it's positive news. Please wait and see what I'm going to tell you." My mum just wanted to know before my father did – no surprise there!

My parents both arrived, and I sat them down and asked them politely if they could hold all questions and comments until I had explained my decision. Both were very surprised, and agreed. I started my

PowerPoint presentation stating that I wished to spend my gap year away in Malawi, as a primary school teacher. At the end of the presentation out of sheer relief and apprehension of what I was about to undertake, and my parent's reaction, I burst into tears looking hopelessly at my family for their approval of my crazy adventure ahead. To my surprise, my parents both smiled and slightly nervously agreed that I could go on my adventure to Malawi, if I promised to come back and go to university afterwards.

The selection process to volunteer with the charity was difficult. It was designed to test a 17-year-old girl and establish if I was able and resilient enough to undertake the challenge of moving to Malawi at the age of 18. I had to fly to Scotland on my own and stay in a hostel overnight, get up at the crack of dawn and catch a ferry over to the small Hebridean island of Coll.

I spent a week on the island with a host family – and no phone signal – to see if I was capable of living in a brand-new country and teach primary school children. I had to fund my own flights, ferry and accommodation to attend the selection and training. To achieve this, I managed to get a job whilst still at school, in a local café, where I worked for several months, to enable me to save the money I needed to attend. This once again, which I didn't realise at the time, demonstrated my resilience and desire for charity work.

I had just turned 18 and a few months later I arrived in the rural, dusty, beautiful country that is Malawi. Malawi is called 'the warm heart of Africa', and lives up to its name, as the people of Malawi are some of the happiest people I have ever met. I arrived in Malawi after a 14-hour flight, a seven-hour bus journey, and no luggage, as it was lost on our connecting flight from Nairobi. I finally arrived at my new home, Mangochi. The culture shock I experienced on arrival was different from what people had said I would feel. I wasn't as homesick as I had originally thought, as I felt for the first time in my life, that I had a purpose on this planet. I could make my own decisions, I could help people in the way I wished, and in the manner I was able to. Not through words and books (as being dyslexic, I had struggled at school) but through my organisational skills and creative mind, that allowed me to engage the children in learning about the many wonders of the world.

The local language was one of the biggest barriers for me. Many people could not speak English, and I felt alone, as communication was difficult. However, I did not let this stop me. I strived every day to learn at least one new word in Chichewa, and of course the main ones, to enable me to understand what the children were saying. After a few months, the once blinding and overwhelming adventure had turned into a place that was very close to my heart.

I was assigned to a standard two class, made up of

children aged between four and seven, with a total of about 45 students. The school day commenced at 7 am, and provided a daily feeding programme, with porridge for each young child. The children would find it difficult to concentrate in class if the meal was not provided, and for some, it would be the only meal that they would be eating that day.

In January 2015, there was heavy flooding in the area, which resulted in famine, as the annual crops were destroyed. This resulted in the school not having access to maize for one week. The children went without food, made worse by the fact that in their normal day-to-day life they couldn't afford food, let alone when prices rose due to famine.

Poverty, starvation and death were things I witnessed in my day-to-day life in Malawi. Resilience, once again, played a part in my life, helping me adapt to culture, language and real life.

After three months of living in a rural village called Bolera, the chief of the village, one of the first female chiefs in the area, asked me if I could help her. I had become familiar with the local language and the chief explained to me that she wanted to learn English. I asked her why; she responded by stating that when she attended meetings with men, they always made decisions without her, because she did not understand English. I agreed, and we started the English lessons the following day. Approximately two weeks later, the women of the village came to me with a problem, they asked, "Why does the chief get to learn English and we don't? We also wish to understand what the men are saying, and get jobs". I responded to the women, why not, let's start school! Everyone in the village and the school I was teaching at thought I was crazy. This had never been done before, but I was inspired by the willingness and desire of the women. I realised that with resilience and enthusiasm, I could attempt to teach the women with the capacity I had. I thought to myself, even if it fails, I must try. From that moment *United Amayi* was born.

To me, Malawian people are some of the most inspirational people in the world. They are positive, happy and live for the present. They experience extreme hardship at times, however, they still celebrate life – and that inspired me. *United Amayi* was established in 2014. Originally it was called Bolera Women's English school (Bolera was the village where the women and I lived). *United Amayi* aims to improve prospects, empower the women and relieve poverty for women through education. *United Amayi* in Chichewa (the Malawian local language) means United Women. Ideally, *United Amayi* aims to create a place where women can feel able to make their own decisions, be empowered and have control over their own lives.

Whilst I was establishing the first women's school in Bolera, and teaching in the primary school, I was also involved in a couple of secondary projects. With the extremely kind donations of people back in Cardiff, we managed to clothe over 1000 children in Bolera village. Every child in the village received a new set of clothing that had been donated from Cardiff. After the flooding, many houses were badly damaged, and with just one coffee morning £300 was raised, which enabled us to rebuild one house and provide two replacement roofs in the village.

Child mortality was something that I really struggled with whilst living in Malawi. One child called Mphatso, really broke my heart. He had been ill for about a year before I arrived. His family hardly had sufficient funds to buy food, let alone afford to take him to the local hospital. One day I managed to catch a bus with him and his mother, and we went to the hospital, to establish if he could be helped. He was diagnosed with kidney problems but a transplant was out of the question as the hospital did not have the capacity to carry out the procedure. They prescribed him medicine that would hopefully make him feel better, and allow him to live the life a four-year-old should be living, one of laughter and joy. In this case, the story had a happy ending. The tablets worked, and Mphatso is now a happy boy, running around and playing with his friends. However, sadly not all the stories of illness ended favourably. This is when not giving up, finding courage, bravery and a glimmer of hope is vital to not get beaten down by the harsh reality of extreme poverty.

The time came for me to leave Malawi after one year living there. It was very sad, and I was determined to make sure that the women's school continued in my absence. I appointed two Malawian ladies to continue teaching the new intake of women.

Four days after arriving back in the UK, I started my studies at the University of Northampton, studying International Development. The first year I was away from the women's school in Malawi was difficult: communication problems, raising funds and needing the time to adapt back into life in the UK. However, after 11 months of the school operating, whilst I was studying in Northampton, I returned to Malawi (my father in tow supporting me) to establish the status of the women's school.

As we approached the dirt track leading down to the village, I hoped with my whole heart, and I turned to my father and said, "Do you think they will remember me?" with a panicked look on my face. My father looked at me, smiled and said, "They will Emma".

The plan for this trip was to expand the school and allow for second year projects. However, the whole trip resulted in resolving the problems that had occurred whilst I was away. Trust needed to be rebuilt, as people didn't believe I would come back and continue the school. However, once stricter policies were introduced and the women saw that I had returned, the original philosophy was reinforced:

to help and empower the women. From then on the school improved greatly.

The last year for *United Amayi* has been outstanding with the opening of a second school in September 2017, the expansion of our curriculum to a two-year programme and job opportunities as an end goal. Whilst back in the UK, multiple fundraising events, including quiz nights, bag packing and grant applications allowed for the two schools to continue. With the new name, we have created a new brochure, website and social media platforms, allowing us to reach a wider audience.

My most recent trip to Malawi, back in summer 2017, opened new doors and opportunities for the expansion of the now charity. We visited the poorest region of Malawi – Nsanje – which affected me greatly. After a four-hour journey down a steep plateau, we arrived in a dusty, barren land, where extreme poverty was rife. We arrived to ascertain if this area was viable to start a new project. It broke my heart to see these people in such extreme poverty and reinforced the reasons I originally established the project: to help the most vulnerable and poverty-stricken women of Malawi.

In 2018, we have a team of five full-time staff in Malawi, ensuring the smooth running and teaching in the two schools. This is confirmation that *United Amayi* is empowering local Malawian women.

Whilst being at the University of Northampton, the incredible support I have received from the Changemaker team, has helped immensely with funding, advice and ongoing support. In the last six months we have won two awards: The *International Recognition* award from the Malawi Association and the *Global Changemaker* award from the University of Northampton. The experience of setting up and running *United Amayi* has been one that has broadened my horizons. I am extremely fortunate that I have found what motivates me, early on in life. Now I can go out and follow my dreams and passions. Without resilience, life can be difficult. People should learn from their mistakes and experiences, and look at them positively, rather than seeing them as a hindrance. Resilience pushes you out of your comfort zone, and allows you to become who you wish to be. So, try it occasionally, do not be too hard on yourself. Take time to reflect on your path and you will realise that you are doing a brilliant job at navigating this thing we call life.

Thank you.

WHO AM I?

Neelam

I am someone who is passionate, determined and I have a can-do attitude towards whatever I undertake. If I make a commitment, I do all that I can to see it through. I am very direct as a person and I believe in saying things as they are, in black and white.

I have many thoughts on the concept of resilience, which I will share below. But I will start with an introduction to who I am and what I have achieved over the years, which has put me in this position to share my story.

I am the Co-Founder and Chairperson of the Indian Hindu Welfare Organisation (IHWO) which was set up in 1996, a multimillion pound project to build a Hindu temple and a Community Centre in Northampton. Martin Luther King famously talked about his dream, and this one is mine.

I was involved with the Northampton Inter-Faith Forum (NIFF) for several years and also elected as a trustee of the National Inter-Faith Network UK.

Over the last 25 years I have been a Founder, Director and Chief Spokesperson for many key organisations and have been featured in several prestigious books and articles as an active member of the community, including Asians *Who's Who* and *Asians of the Millennium*.

I have extensive experience of the local health economy, having previously been a Non-Executive Director with various NHS Trusts.

I have also held positions as a Vice-Chair of the PCT, a Co-Chair of the BME Sub-Regional Partnership and a Lay Member of the Lord Chancellor Advisory Committee. Most recently, I have completed my nine-year term as an advisory committee member and have now been appointed to the Northamptonshire bench as a Magistrate and look forward to this new chapter.

Many people may find it hard to believe that I started out my career in retail. Everything I have done and built has been from hard work and nothing else.

I have been fortunate enough to be awarded an MBE in 2013 and made Deputy Lieutenant of Northamptonshire in 2014. I was also given the *Anne Frank Award* for my contribution to education and was awarded the very first *Inspirational Woman of the Year* in 2013. I am truly humbled to have received such honours and continue to strive in my work and commitments.

My experience with 'resilience'

Resilience is defined as *the capacity to recover quickly from difficulties.*

I sat down and thought about this definition for some time, but something wasn't quite sitting right with me. I believe most of us, whether we realise it or not, have the capacity for things. I also believe that resilience is ultimately demonstrated in that process of recovering from difficulty, whatever that difficulty may be. I suppose that my challenge is with the word 'quickly'. We are all in a rush in life, to get over things. Quickly. To deal with problems. Quickly. To find solutions to problems. Quickly.

I would argue that resilience is not a question of speed and how quickly you can recover from a difficulty. In the long term, I don't think speedy recoveries are that healthy. Doing it quickly is like putting a plaster on a wound and then walking on. No. Regardless of capacity to recover, or the speed with which you do so, I believe that resilience is about the courage you demonstrate in facing a difficulty, and the patience and empathy you show to yourself while recovering from it. For me, that's what real resilience has meant in context – in my own life and in the great stories of others which I have seen and been a part of.

The latter part about showing patience and empathy to yourself is something that it took me a long time to realise. I have always felt that it is important to put others first because that is selfless. It is. I thought the by-product of this was that putting yourself first was self*ish*. This is where I went wrong. If I'm not ok, what good am I to others and to those people that I put before me? How effective can I really be? Putting yourself first isn't always selfish, sometimes it's just the sensible thing to do. You can operate more effectively and efficiently and that's when you're then in a good position to help others. So that's showing yourself empathy, but what about patience?

Although I can't speak for others, I do feel that us women often place very demanding expectations on ourselves, based on what we think we *should* be able to do or *need* to do. We expect that we should be able to get over things quickly and get on with it; we tell ourselves that we need to stop dwelling otherwise we are weak; we expect that we should be able to deal with everything by ourselves because that's what makes us strong women. But who decided these things? Where did we get these ideas from? If one of our girlfriends were in our situation, I wonder whether we would be telling them that they should be doing those things. If we wouldn't, why do we think it's ok to say it to ourselves? Why are we not kinder with ourselves? This is why I think resilience is there in the patience you show yourself too. Because to be patient with yourself means to also have the courage to stick your hand up against these ideas and expectations that we think we *should* be placing on ourselves.

Despite my perspective on this now, life has often handed me a set of circumstances where I had no choice but to recover quickly from the difficulty. I'm not a unique case. I have realised that a lot of people find themselves in this position, whereby they need to just 'get on with things' because life's priorities take over. So you just have to put on some lipstick, smile and walk out of the door with a positive attitude.

Often, the reason for having to take this approach involves some kind of responsibility towards another person or people. In my case, sometimes it was my parents and siblings, sometimes my children or other times members of the community, that were dependent on me taking certain decisions and making that quick recovery. Sometimes, people weren't even aware that I had something to recover from!

And society tells you that strong people get on with things – they don't sit and dwell.

I am so honoured to have an opportunity to tell my story in this book. Because I am an inspirational woman and I have worked hard to get where I have gotten to – but people only hear of you at the point where you have reached a stage of success. No one knew who I was when I worked for Marks & Spencer. It is often labelled as the perfectionist problem for young people, who see success stories, but don't see the setbacks that had to be overcome for the person to get there, and so they end up with an unrealistic view of what the journey to success involved and lose motivation or constantly criticise themselves because they can't seem to get there quickly enough in their own eyes.

My days at Marks & Spencer were long and repetitive, but I really enjoyed working there and the interactions I'd have with my colleagues. In those days, I spoke little English and a broken marriage had left me believing that I really wouldn't be going anywhere significant in my life. But that didn't matter, because I had never comprehended any different. I was just wrapped up in doing what I needed to in order to make ends meet.

As I write this, it almost seems unbelievable to me that I went from my small world working in Marks & Spencer to being awarded an MBE – an award given by the Queen – and being appointed as a Deputy Lieutenant for Northamptonshire, nearly 25 years later. So much has happened over those years and I have been blessed with wonderful opportunities and progress in my career. As a firm believer of giving back – even before you've got it – much of my time has been dedicated to the voluntary sector. I co-founded the Indian Hindu Welfare Organisation (IHWO), a charity that was originally set up in 1996. We have ambitious plans to build a Hindu temple and community centre in Northampton, catering for local residents from cradle to grave, and this multimillion pound project was officially launched in the House of Commons. It is my belief in my creator and in the principles of giving back and helping others that I have grown up with that really drive me in this area. There is so much fulfilment and satisfaction I derive from helping others, and it is something unique as a feeling, that doesn't come from anything else. Selfless service has been a core principle of my upbringing and my life and I am forever grateful to my parents for all that they have taught me about this.

I have also particularly enjoyed my work in the education sector, where I was instrumental in facilitating better relationships between parents and schools, as part of the Northampton Excellence Cluster. This, along with many other work endeavours across faith, health, leadership coaching and the community, has really brought me a wealth of experience in understanding and empathising with people from many different walks of life and helped me to reflect on my own life in a way which is constructive and meaningful.

I mention this because I am in a place now where I notice, more than ever, the breadth of suffering and difficulty that people around me and including me encounter, whether due to ill health, death of a loved one, challenges with children or something along those lines. There are two things that are common: one being that they never fail to shock you; and the second being an acceptance that the last time this happened is never the last time. Events or discoveries on a single day can change the course of your lifetime and this is just how things are, perhaps it is the test of God.

In the midst of all of this, I sometimes close my eyes and various questions enter my mind. What is the purpose of all of this? The success and the suffering? What does it all lead to? How should I be handling these things? Am I handling them correctly? Am I *really* resilient?

The last one is definitely one that recently popped into my mind, when I was asked to share my story as an inspirational woman. I am sure that many women out there do show a lot of resilience, but don't recognise or acknowledge themselves for having done so. So I wanted to share four key indicators that I believe make it very clear that you are someone who demonstrates resilience. And I sincerely hope that many others, like me, will read these, relate to them and credit themselves with the praise they deserve for being people of resilience.

1. **Doing it on a tough day.** 'It' refers to whatever that thing is that you need to do – it could be anything from going into work, to making time to help someone, going to the gym or taking your children somewhere. We all have those days where something intervenes, either mentally or physically, and we just want to resign ourselves to our bed. When you perform on those days where only you know it's tougher than usual, you demonstrate

an acceptance that you aren't always going to be feeling ready and up to scratch when you need to perform – but you know you can still do it despite that. It takes some confidence, but it makes some confidence too.

2. Having heart. When you do go and perform on a tough day, or you do the thing you need to do in general, don't be surprised if further setbacks come in your way and suddenly it is being made even harder for you. It feels unjust and you want to scream and shout but this is where it is important to have heart. It's that attitude where you say *"go on, throw your worst at me – I'm still going to get through it, and get through it well"*. You can often surprise yourself in these situations because you are being tested at the point that you think there is nothing left in the tank. But somehow and from somewhere, you manage to find the energy and strength to do it. That's the resilience in you.

3. Empathising with the enemy. I don't literally mean the enemy in this instance. I am referring to the person that you don't have anything good to say about in the situation or that you view as a rival. A difficult colleague, a person that has it easier than you, someone that is always outperforming you, an ignorant person – whoever it may be. Despite whatever your feelings may be towards the person, whether rational or not, when you are able to acknowledge those feelings and still consider their perspective or situation and do the right thing by them, that shows fine character. It shows that you are able to rise above things and still act in accordance with what you believe in, as opposed to being swayed by situations. It demonstrates composure and it requires resilience, because it is testing you against the voice which is trying to tell you otherwise.

4. Doing it for yourself first. I mentioned this previously because I feel this really is one of the key points to understand in becoming a resilient person and sustaining yourself as one. Moving away from an idea that doing things for yourself first is selfish, is not easy. You may also face resistance along the way, if it is an idea you have grown up with. That is why it shows you are resilient when you can do the right thing by yourself in order to then do the right thing by others. Giving others importance does not mean giving yourself less or none. If we talk about equality, this should begin with where we sit in our own minds, against others – whether strangers, acquaintances or our own families. Not doing it for yourself first is a bit like not putting enough petrol in the car tank, and still expecting that it will get everyone to their destination. At some point the car will break down, right?

There have been points in my life where I have fallen victim to all of the above. But that's the whole point and that's why I am writing this story now. Because I have fallen victim, but I have believed and tried again. I want to say that I have come out on the other side but, as I mentioned before, the last time is never the last time. Life is a constant trial, and I just have sharper tools in my box now.

This has reminded me of something very profound written by Malcolm X in his autobiography:

Children have a lesson adults should learn, to not be ashamed of failing, but to get up and try again. Most of us adults are so afraid, so cautious, so "safe", and therefore so shrinking and rigid and afraid that it is why so many humans fail. Most middle-aged adults have resigned themselves to failure.

Being resilient is not an award you are handed. It is not something you get and then never need to work for again. Resilience comes from you in moments and stays in those moments. And every time we are faced with new situations, we have to make conscious decisions as to what we want to do and what we want to show, to ourselves and to others.

We have the capacity and we are often enough presented with the difficulty. So we are just left with a decision – and that decision is ours to make.

It is my own experience and observation that women in the main face a lot of challenges in our society and, in particular, as a woman from a male-dominated culture, I have found the challenges to be greater. Added to that, the challenges I have faced as a single parent and an ethnic minority and a divorcee, in a culture where divorce was unheard of. And then going on to become a woman that leads and directs and decides, having come from a culture which has taught me how to be subservient. I have faced a lot of opposition along the way, and it has been most difficult when the opposing people were people that I love. But through determination I have overcome such challenges and you can too. Whatever those challenges may be, you can rise above them and come out on top of things. You can see success and you can do it without compromising who you are, and still ultimately gain the support of good people around you.

I have realised that you have to just keep striving in life. And if you have the belief, nothing can stop you. It is true that challenges will come in your way, but it is also true that you will find solutions for them. Then more things will come in your way and you will find solutions again. Once you believe and accept that, you will find that all those things that once seemed impossible are not only possible, but already in progress. And it is you that will make them happen and see them through.

It always starts and ends with you. As Gandhi said, *you* have to be the change you wish to see in the world.

MY STORY

Life can be a beautiful experience but at the same time an endless rollercoaster. It's the experiences in life that help us through each step which can either break or make us. Sometimes we have to fall in order to come back up again but the most important thing is to never give up and understand that everything happens for a reason no matter how hard that may seem at the time. The story you are about to read is not a cheerful one but it is what made me into the person I am today.

I was born in Europe in the late 1980s into a mixed race family and had parents who followed two different religions. I knew being a woman or a girl at the time was going to be a difficult experience from the very beginning. I was the eldest of three daughters but I never got the opportunity to grow up with my sisters properly. When I was four years old I came to England for a family holiday with my two-year-old sister and parents. After the holiday my father left my sister in England to live with my uncle and his family, I did not see her until eight years later and by then she saw me as her 'cousin' rather than her sister. My youngest sister was born with Down's syndrome and I spent five years with her before I was dropped off in England with my auntie and her family aged ten at the time.

I have various memories of the first ten years of my life. I remember being dressed up as a boy and my father treating me like a boy. I was told often that he wished I was a boy and he would never recover from the fact that he was granted with three daughters and no sons. I knew from that moment onwards that no matter what I did I could never make my father happy. I was not allowed to go on school trips or participate in school plays, any extra-curricular activity was forbidden, so instead I spent most of my time at home and cycling when my father was at work. School life was good but I was bullied due to my mixed race and called various names which knocked my confidence.

As my father worked 12 hours a day my mother decided to send me to my local gymnasium without my father's knowledge so I could learn gymnastics. As the years progressed I started competing in gymnastics at a national level and remember winning numerous medals up until the age of ten before I moved to England.

Overall the first ten years of my life were good but I also witnessed a lot of domestic violence and this is what changed a lot of my thinking of life overall and convinced me that being a girl was not a good thing. It also brought hatred for religion within my heart as I assumed that it was religion that taught my father to be the way he was. I remember going to the mosque on a Friday and church on a Sunday all of which at the time was very confusing. Despite these challenges the love for singing, acting and competing in gymnastics helped me forget my struggles.

At the age of ten I came to England once again for a family holiday and before I knew it my father decided to leave me here with my auntie and her family. From that moment onwards my whole life changed and I knew my dream of singing, acting and gymnastics was all over. Imagine being left in a new country without your parents, you don't know any English or the languages your relatives spoke. You are not allowed to contact your parents and there is no one who can understand what you are going through.

I spent 6 months at home doing the chores and living life in fear from the moment I woke up in the morning till the moment I went to bed at night before I was enrolled into primary school. I once again was the subject of hatred as I came from a mixed background which wasn't acceptable within the house I lived in. For this reason I was told that I wasn't good enough, I was weak, I wasn't intelligent and I will never achieve anything in life, I am just a waste of space and didn't deserve anything good. The authorities in this country are corrupt and therefore there was no one who could help me i.e. the police, which I sadly believed for 11 years. From that moment onwards I lost all faith in people and trusting people became very difficult and at times still is today.

I remember being in Year 6 and learning my ABC and spellings whilst the rest of my class were preparing for their upcoming SATs but the beauty of starting school is that I saw hope. This was the first time since moving to England I had people of my age trying to help me in class and making sure I wasn't alone during break times. It showed me that there were nice people in this country and no matter how difficult it seemed at the time there was light at the end of the tunnel. Home life was still difficult, I never got time to study or do things that children at my age did and this continued throughout my teenage years.

I remember being the subject of child abuse, hate, modern slavery, forced marriage and honour based violence which lead to wanting to commit suicide when I was 14 years old on numerous occasions. I attempted suicide a number of times but for various reasons I was unsuccessful. Then I found faith and at that point I learned that it was not worth it, not to forget that suicide was forbidden in my chosen faith.

My high school life was everything to me and whilst other children loved the weekend and holidays, I hated them. School life showed me that there is a good world out there and I got the opportunity to meet some lovely people. It is because of them that I am still here today.

Once I had found faith I decided to deal with my problems at home through prayer and I started writing my own diary for a few years. My diary was my best friend and I would write how each day went. Despite my language barriers and not being able to commit time to my studies I sat 10 GCSEs whilst at high school, but as expected I was unable to achieve a high grade, although I did pass them all. This did not matter to my relatives as they had made it clear that once I had left high school I was not allowed to study any further or get a paid job but instead they made plans for a forced marriage. Fortunately I survived as my European passport had expired for a long time and despite trying to get it renewed they failed on numerous occasions.

After high school I once again was homebound for over a year with no money or social life but I had my faith which gave me hope. Eventually I became a financial burden on my relatives because they no longer received any child benefit for me so I was allowed to enrol onto an apprentice course. As I didn't achieve the required GCSE grade for English and Maths I started from the bottom with a Level 1 NVQ in Business Administration. Over the years I worked my way up the education ladder part-time whilst working full-time. I was 17 years old when my parents moved to England. I lived without my parents for seven years and now I was living with them back again as a teenager having forgotten my mother tongue language and leading a religious life which instantly lead to clashes.

The vicious circle of living without freedom and having my life controlled continued. Over the next four years despite the struggles I continued with my studies and working career and eventually managed to sort out my passport, driving licence, passed my driving test and bought a car by myself. This irritated my father to a point where I was the subject of honour based violence and started receiving death threats. I left home on two separate occasions after which I returned on my relatives' request but soon realised that my relatives had no interest in my safety, they were just trying to protect their family name.

On the third occasion I was taken away by the police as things got much worse. I was homeless for 8 weeks before I was able to afford rented accommodation. Having earned for a number of years most of my finances were spent for charity purposes leaving very little for myself. I always wanted to do things for others but hardly thought about my future. I lived the next four years of my life by myself, in fear of my own life as I couldn't leave the town my father and his family lived in due to financial reasons. I was disowned by my own family and my mother and sister moved into a refuge 30 miles away.

I felt lonely for a very long time which was very

challenging both mentally and emotionally but I still didn't give up on life once, no matter how difficult it might have been. This was due to my faith, friends and work colleagues who helped me through each step mentally. I now had freedom and could live life the way I wanted to and built a career as an ICT software consultant. Eventually I got married and moved to Northampton over five years ago. I have had to re-start my career from scratch as I was unable to find a job in the same field. I started working in public safety and have worked my way up the ladder.

Moving town has been a big test and the loss of three children has not made it easy but my previous challenges have made me a stronger person and I have shown myself that I can get through it with patience. I am now fortunate enough to be a mother to a beautiful three-year-old, and a wife to a wonderful husband who has shown me that there are good men out there. I am currently studying a master's degree as I want to be a living example to my own child and prove to myself that those who doubted me were wrong and will always be wrong.

This was a small glimpse of my life to show you that not everything is perfect in life but the good stuff will always outweigh the bad stuff. I could sit here cursing those who hurt me and made my childhood a misery but instead I have decided to forgive them and move on because I want to live my life instead of allowing a few narrow-minded people to destroy it. No matter what people may say to you, never stop believing in yourself. Life is a test and for a woman slightly bigger, but no matter what life throws at us we *will* get through it.

Finally, *never* change yourself for someone else; there is nothing much greater than to just be you.

YOUR MISSION

A young Indian woman reflects on her life, on her civil marriage and finds herself starry eyed, looking at the young man she had just married after only their second meeting.

She could not believe how modern and fun the in-laws seemed in contrast to her own reserved family. The tradition of an arranged marriage was instilled right from the start of teenage years by her very traditional family that put their family respect in the eyes of others above everything else. The childhood, although loving and caring, it was simple and strict, there were rare outings or after school activities, the main focus was on family life. Primary school was horrendous with racist remarks, being left out of group work and even one young boy constantly bullying by standing at the stairs and threatening to push her down. The racism and feelings of isolation from the outside world led to an unconfident and quiet young girl. However, things started to change once she started college and started driving at age 19. Her interests grew in pop music, going out and shopping, life became fun. Gaining her first job meant financial independence too, she could feel the loss of control with the new-found freedom.

The search for a 'match' started at 20 years of age and proved to be a most uncomfortable experience, when each potential groom's family inspected her like a piece of meat with their critical eye. Everything from the tone of her skin colour to her height and other credentials such as education and expectations of marrying the family as well as the son. The match did not quite meet the promises that her father had initially made, however, the talk of all the positives about the quiet handsome young man, a respectable well to do family and the glitz of the wedding plans helped the naïve young woman to just follow the flow without questioning. The exciting big fat Indian wedding day came and all she could think about was – how would she cope with being far away from her caring family? A family that had always wrapped their first-born child in cotton wool and even spoilt her. Her reservations were to be proved correct.

From the first day, she knew she would never fit in, the overpowering large family seemed to be more traditional and strict than even her own. There were high expectations as a daughter-in-law to provide everything for all the extended family as they had become accustomed to in the past – to ask for permission to do anything, to lose all independence and be selfless. Comments were made about appearance, guilt if she sat down to relax, pressure to have a child, silly games to make her look unintelligent, although the family had substantial issues themselves, the negative focus was always in her. The silent treatment was given, if she went out with her husband or if she wanted to visit her parents she was even told, "You shouldn't have got married if you wanted to stay at your parents". Although the husband was most loving, he could not do much to help and even struggled himself with constant criticism. She could not do anything to please them, so she went back to the quiet unconfident young girl from primary school; she had no freedom, no status and eventually realised she was mentally drained. She felt that the circumstances may have arisen, without any ill intent from anyone, that may be it was just tradition and culture and that she just did not fit in, she told herself it was no one's fault.

Things became more bearable when she had her first born, she had a new life to live for and the love of a baby that would get her through. She promised her baby girl the world and that she would be brought up with everything that was lacking from her own life. A few years later she had another daughter, now she was made to feel like an unwanted baby and the mother to feel as if it was her fault for producing another girl instead of a boy. Unable to cope with the expectations and demands, she finally broke and left home to return to her parents, this was the ultimate shame for the family.

After a week, she returned.

At this point she convinced her husband to break the tradition of living with the extended family and to buy a home of their own. With this new found confidence she was able to find a well-paid part time job to begin saving for a new home. However, even this job was not without struggles, bringing back painful memories of school, where colleagues were constantly bickering and back stabbing each other. She realised it was time for a new chapter, to leave work and home. Although moving out was yet another act of disrespect, the tables were set to turn and forgiveness was received from both sides.

The fresh start was a dream come true for the young family, to have their own space, freedom to live how they wanted to and not to be constantly watched and judged. Having a new home and young family resulted in financial issues, but she finally had some peace of mind, which was way more valuable than money. She bought a picture of a peace lily, mounting it on the wall to signify their new tranquil space. An opportunity arose for a job within a community setting and it brought a small income and opportunity to have an interest outside of home. Although things now seemed perfect, further issues began to arise.

Now that there were no extended family issues to deal with, she noticed things about her husband more now: the need for control, shouting, aggressiveness, excessive alcohol and other totally unacceptable behaviour, which is too painful to mention. The more she noticed it, the more she searched for answers and tried to confront it.

The next few years were full of arguments, blame, verbal and physical abuse and alcohol abuse. She was made to look like she was in the wrong, by telling lies about her to both families and friends. The games continued but she did not lose hope and carried on battling to save her marriage. One thing that kept her busy and afloat was her work but even that became stressful at times due to politics. As each situation worsened, she threw herself more and more into work.

The difference with the new work was that it always lead to the aim of supporting people. She realised that her story was in fact the story of many around her, she realised she was not suffering alone and her own experiences opened her eyes. From then on, each initiative was about providing support, tackling inequality, confidence building and issues awareness. The task ahead was not easy, as some of the people she worked with had cultural barriers that they struggled to break out of and the new vision would cause controversy. The risk did not deter her and she had the support family and friends, encouraging her to do what was right for those who needed support and without fear. Many of the new initiatives were successful in achieving their aims and some gained recognition.

Additionally, the promise of raising strong independent forward thinking young girls was nearly accomplished. One of the thoughtful daughters wrote a bucket list to help her at one of her lowest points; it included everything from professional development, learning new skills to having regular fun. Her sibling encouraged her towards personal development and to have faith. The resulting bucket list and personal development journey both helped to transform what was once a victim into a strong independent woman who was able to support others. Various training opportunities provided a platform to not only support people with issues but also her personal life issues. Personal development provided confidence and skills to understand and deal with any situation head on. Even having fun assisted to keep things in perspective – the family and friends you have fun with, you identify their issues and needs, always share your stories as everyone is going through a similar journey to yours!

The more issues she faced the more fire ignited and the more passion flowed to not only be strong herself but make a difference, to make change for others with your own journey! Sometimes you go through challenges and then you realise it was for a reason, it was *your mission* – God chose you to experience the negatives as he knows you are strong enough to survive and passionate enough to help others going through the same.

Stephanie

Staring blankly at the bare walls of my room, I cast my mind back to a few years previously. My stomach sinking, and a heavy, looming sense of confusion and despair hanging over me. I thought back to the hot summery days; during my time as an undergraduate. Going for long walks around green parks, enjoying the lush scenery, warm air, and being out with nature.

I imagined a time where I was always smiling. I remember that I used to smile so much, my cheeks would be sore, and was laughing for much of my time when I was with others. I was ambitious, loved the outdoors and actively sought to get involved in local community groups.

I blinked slowly. My eyes heavy, with a slight tinge of red from exhaustion, and my eyelids damp from where I had been tearful. Back in reality. A reality that reflected a starkly opposite memory. Sitting still, those memories faded away, and I was back in the moment; still staring at the bare walls.

Where had all those happy times and memories gone?

How had I ended up in this state where I am constantly tearful and upset?

What was it like to be happy?

These questions circulated in my head repeatedly. I could not think; could not even function. I was as lifeless as the bare walls that surrounded me.

I was trapped. Alone. Isolated. Stuck with an ever-changing form that dominated my thoughts, emotions and ability to function. Dragging me through a bottomless pit; an eternal black hole; where no one else knew of my existence. Bad memories played on repeat in my head; fostering a growing sense of self-loathing and igniting an untamed anger.

It had been going on for months and months. A restless burden hanging on my shoulders, where a raging storm in my head screamed into my ears. All I could hear were the voices of bad memories clinging to my ear drums, blocking out all sound from what was going on around me. My anger grew and grew, and my sleeping patterns, sense of self and identity changed.

In my gut, I knew that I was no longer the same person I was. How strange it seemed, that, when thinking back to the way I was two years ago; I was in a state of constant happiness and content; now, I could barely smile without hiding behind the mental chaos that plagued my wellbeing.

When did all this start?

Why is this happening to me?
Will I ever get over this?
What is it?

Whilst I remained still, I wondered when all this emotional and mental turmoil started. I thought long and hard, as to how, from being a cheerful individual to someone in a state of constantly being low and tearful.

January 2016 came; and I experienced it for the first time then. Multiple bad memories were happening in that instant. A wave of past events hit me like a ton of bricks, and I broke down. This was not only on this one occasion in January; but a regular occurrence that grew over the months.

I started back at university on a very positive note; I had passed all of my modules with good grades, and had been offered two new jobs; a great start to the New Year and second term of my master's.

February

Once January had ended, I was still surprised as to how I was still feeling low and agitated all the time. It made no sense to me. I didn't think much of it in January,

March

April

May

There was a sharp snap and a rope pulled up. Looking downwards, a pair of legs dangled, and a lifeless body hung. A sudden flash, and a coffin was lowered into the ground. By the coffin, a group of people, devastated, staring in shock and disbelief, watched as the coffin was lowered into the ground. Another flash; and the image pierced me. I curled up, sobbing profusely. No longer wanting to carry this heinous burden with me, I sought help.

Building Resilience

The proceeding weeks went quickly, and I found myself battling against the odd depressive storm. My motivation had picked up, and I was feeling much more like myself again. Whilst everything seemed to be picking up; I endeavoured to push myself that little bit more for self-recovery, and to find my own feet and develop my own coping mechanisms.

I don't want to be on medication forever. I need to find a new way of helping myself get through this, and not be so dependent on the medication.

CITIZENSHIP

Rumbi

I have recently attended my British Citizenship Ceremony and started to reflect on the journey. It's been a long journey. I have learnt many lessons and thought to share my part of my journey. It's in three parts. I know that many people will relate to the challenges that I have faced. Many are still going through the process and will find encouragement from our story.

A part of my journey so far that has perhaps been the most difficult to deal with has been my migration to the UK. I left Zimbabwe with my husband in tears. My husband was coming here to study. He initially came on his own and left me and Tino in Zimbabwe. He left me working at a lawyers' firm located in the Avenues in Harare. We were both miserable. I was miserable in Zimbabwe and he was miserable in London. He came back to Zimbabwe after experiencing depression and missing his new family. We discussed his future and decided as a family that Muchada and I should return to the UK and leave Tino. This was one of most heart-wrenching and painful experiences in my life. Tino was my new born, my beautiful son. I met him on 11 January 1998 and fell instantly in love with the handsome little man. I had not even weaned him and gave him his last breast milk at the airport. I cried all the way to the UK. We had to leave him because we were going to the unknown world of London. We had £100 and two sleeping bags when we arrived in London. My in-laws felt that taking a child to the UK in those circumstances was not safe and was irresponsible. My mother-in-law and my father-in-law had lived in the UK in the seventies and knew that we would struggle in the UK with a small child.

We reluctantly agreed with all the words of wisdom. I felt that I owed it to my husband to support him in his bid to further his education in the UK. I felt guilty because I had stopped him from going to pursue his studies when I fell pregnant. He had disappointed his parents and he owed it to them to pursue his dreams and to use the money that had been paid for his school fees as it was non-refundable. I had worked for a few years but felt that it was better to give it a go and come to the UK with him.

I left my son and cried all the way to Gatwick airport. My brother cried when he left me at the airport. He was devastated that I was going to this unknown world, devastated that I was leaving my career. My parents were disappointed that I was going to London with no plan. As far as they could see I was just following my husband. They had wanted me to pursue my career as a lawyer and settle down well in my life.

I left Harare airport in turmoil and in tears. We arrived in the UK with three telephone numbers for people who could help us with accommodation. When we arrived at Gatwick airport we caught the tube to Victoria Station. We started phoning people who might be able to accommodate us. The first lady who we telephoned told us that we could sleep in her lounge but only for one night. We tried another number and the lady told us that she could not help us. We had one number left. We telephoned the Machisa family. There was no answer on their landline. We bought some bananas at a shop at the station. I will never forget the bananas because of the colour they were bright yellow and perfectly shaped. I could not get over their perfection. It seems random but I was used to yellow and black bananas which were oddly shaped. We decided to try calling the Machisa's again later. We called their house at 7pm and were delighted when they answered. Mr Machisa sounded very friendly and told us to come straight away. They had a spare room and were happy to accommodate us. We hired a black mini cab from Victoria Station to Peckham. We did not even realise how expensive it was but were afraid to get lost in the London underground. We lived with them for the first five months of our stay in the UK.

To say I was disappointed would be a gross understatement. I expected London, England to be a place full of white English people like those I had seen in the films. I expected to see white picket fences and quaint cottages. I expected to see grand beautiful houses. I was surprised to see so many "black" people from all over the world. I was surprised to see dirty streets and identical houses. I could barely understand what the people were saying to me. They did not sound like they were speaking in English. London was a culture shock for me. It was cold and miserable. The people did not even smile and walked fast all the time.

I struggled to get a job and was quickly told to forget pursuing a career in law. I struggled so much and fell into what I can now only describe as a depression. I cried so much. I missed my little boy terribly. I felt so guilty for leaving him in Zimbabwe. I found it difficult to live with strangers and really struggled to settle down. I found work quickly at a nursing agency called "Delta". I did not know what the work was until my first shift. I arrived at a nursing home and recall being told to toilet the residents. I had no clue, no experience and did not even know what to do. I retched at the sight of a resident's pad. I had only ever changed my son's nappy and had never looked after an elderly person. I was so shocked at the thought that this is what I had left Zimbabwe to come and do. I felt dirty and washed my hands continuously trying to remove the smell of faeces. I smelt it on my clothes, in my hair – everywhere. I could not eat or drink; everywhere I went I smelt the distinct nursing home smells.

I vividly recall my first few months in the UK as if it were yesterday. I cried and cried and cried so many times. I blamed my husband for bringing me to the UK. I felt that it was his fault that I had to do all this menial work and suffer in the cold. I recall waking up in the dark at 5 am to catch the bus and the Tube to work for a 7 am start. I would then return home at 9 pm after finishing at 7 pm. I did not even get to see the sunshine. I found life in England very depressing and lonely.

I recall once when we had no bus fare and my husband had to walk from Peckham to Central London where he was working as a kitchen porter. He walked a good three hours in the cold. He walked a good two hours one way. I was able to plait someone's hair and got twenty pounds. I recall the tangible relief on his face when I went to pick him up from his place of work.

Our marriage suffered greatly at this time and for years to follow. We stayed together by the grace of God. I had always lived in a country where I had family support and was familiar with everyone and everything. In England I was displaced and felt disenfranchised. I was told that I would have to forget about my law degree and do nursing like everyone else. My husband

and I both had a choice of doing nursing. Our host, Mrs Machisa, advised us both to apply and attend the interviews. She gave us sound practical advice. She advised us that if we studied nursing then we would be able to live in this country permanently. I decided to apply for nursing and was offered a place at Stoke Mandeville Hospital. I wanted to return to Zimbabwe to collect my son but my mother-in-law told me that she was going to bring him to London and that there was no need for me to come back.

My son joined us after a separation of five months. We were again the more fortunate ones. In my work in assisting migrants regularise their immigration status I have heard heartbreaking stories of families separated. Parents separated from their children for more than a decade. There is a whole generation of children that have grown up without their parents. The economic collapse in Zimbabwe caused many people to migrate to first world countries in search of a better future. This migration caused the break-up of numerous families and many children ended up being raised by grandparents. Our reunification with our son was a chance for a new beginning for us. I could not continue to study nursing. I was not motivated to do so. I therefore left nursing with the plan that my husband would use his maths and physics qualification to pursue a career in teaching.

In the early 2000s the political and economic situation in Zimbabwe declined at an alarming rate.

Zimbabwe began experiencing a period of considerable political and economic upheaval in 1999. Opposition to President Mugabe and the ZANU-PF government grew considerably after the mid-1990s in part due to worsening economic and human rights conditions.

Zimbabwe's economic crisis precipitated an exodus of professionals and skilled workers emigrating in search of better economic opportunities.

Whilst in the UK our family informed us that the situation in Zimbabwe had rapidly declined on both a political and economic level and therefore it was better for us to stay on in the UK. Our family in Zimbabwe advised us not to return to Zimbabwe but to stay in the UK. We stayed on and extended our leave to remain.

We then started the struggle of dealing with the Home Office in a bid to get permanent residence in the UK (known as Indefinite Leave to Remain). Our immigration history was quite standard. Initially we had been students and then my husband switched to a work permit visa.

I worked in the industrial areas and in the care industry for a few years. It was the most frustrating existence that I had ever faced. I wanted to return to Zimbabwe but could not go back. I recall once sitting in the middle of a dual carriageway in tears. I felt that the situation on the road represented my life. I was stuck between a rock and a hard place. I found the life in the UK depressing and I was not using my God-given abilities. I was frustrated working in the care industry. I could not see myself returning to Zimbabwe either. I saw cars in front of me and cars behind me. The picture on the dual carriageway depicted my life and the place where I was at that particular time. I was so devastated and just saw no way out. The future seemed bleak.

I had made so many applications to agencies for work as a lawyer and to law firms. I received rejection after rejection. When the post came the people in my house would laugh and say "It's Rumbi's regrets". I felt so rejected and so downcast. My parents.

I recall going to Extra Personnel in Coventry and looking for a secretarial job. I failed the typing test dismally. The recruitment agent even made me do the test again and my score was still dismal. They told me that they would keep my details on file and if anything came up they would let me know. I recall the day that I went to enter Extra Personnel Office rather than Industry; I had worked up the courage and had taken the very bold step of going to the Office side. My mind had been reconditioned to think that I could not work in an office and could only work in industry or care. My self-confidence and self-esteem had taken a great knock. I had started to believe what everyone else was saying. I tried to conform to the environment and let the environment dictate my destiny.

Taking that step to wear a suit and enter Extra Personnel Office Placements changed the course that my career would take. One day whilst sleeping on my bed and sobbing (I cried a lot), my mobile rang. I ignored the call as it was an anonymous number. The call came through again. I was offered a job as an enquiries officer at the Law Society.

I was getting paid £6 per hour. After three months my manager Pat encouraged me to apply for a permanent caseworker position. I made the application and my salary jumped to £17,000, with private medical care, gym membership and all the perks. I managed to convert my legal qualifications and qualified as Solicitor with the help of the Law Society.

I worked well in my job. I made great friends and really felt settled. We bought a house and had two children during my time at the Law Society. I always had a desire to open up my own law practice and worked hard to do so.

I established and opened a solicitor's practice in faith and in the belief that I would have my settlement papers in the UK. I started a solicitor's practice at The Quadrant in Coventry. I established and opened this practice in faith. It was a giant leap of faith moving from my comfortable and secure job at the Law Society to practise as a sole practitioner. I was encouraged and inspired to set up a practice serving the Zimbabwean community by one of my pastors in Forward in Faith. Pastor Mudere preached in Coventry a message about "creating a bosom" and allowing God to bless us .He encouraged the congregation to step out in faith and to go for their dreams. He encouraged us to become employers in this foreign nation and to go for gold. I still recall the day as if it was yesterday. The congregation was standing and cheering. It was a powerful and motivating message. I left the meeting with no motivation; I had been caught up in the euphoria of the moment and enjoyed the message but I was thinking he is preaching to the others. The next day Pastor Mudere phoned me and said "Mama, I was preaching to you as well, you need to let go of your fear." The encouragement that I received from this pastor led me to think of starting my own practice.

My friends encouraged me; Jaimie and Nyarai Garande encouraged me to start the practice and to break out and aspire for more. I distinctly recall Jaimie driving a 60-mile round trip to try and encourage me to think outside the box. His way of encouraging was unconventional. He tried to motivate me by telling me how well he was doing. I sent him a long email telling him off for showing off to me. I had a very long rant. Bless him! It's good to have good friends because he ignored my rant and left me. I can only say the Lord continued to minister to me. I had a very good work colleague, Muz Khan. He encouraged me to set up and even promised to invest some money in the business. Hannah and Andy encouraged me and helped me to write a business plan. Rose and Shepherd gave me my first computer and encouraged me to just get on with it.They were all such encouragers in my life. Muz pulled out the day I handed in my resignation!

Muz encouraged me to start and to draw up my business plan and held my hand along the way, knowing that after I had taken the plunge he would leave me to fly on my own. I still think he had more faith than me. As my friend he saw the gold that was in me but knew that I was too frightened to do it on my own. He saw potential in me that sadly I did not see in myself. He walked alongside me for a season and a reason. It reminds me of the time that my brother taught me to ride a bicycle. He pushed me and reassured me but knew that he would need to let go. When he let go I was able to ride on my own. Looking back I felt doubt and fear. The same thing happened in my business; I never thought I could do it on my own so needed someone to hold onto.

I learnt a valuable lesson during this season of my life. It's important to have people who bring out the best in you and encourage you to believe in yourself. I needed to have that push to go for my dreams. I changed from being an employee to an employer.

Fear was a big thing for me. I was afraid to step out. I was afraid of failure. I was afraid of the financial problems that I felt that I would face. I feared leaving the job security and becoming my own boss. I loved my job at the Law Society. It was secure; I was paid a very good salary and was established. I worked from home for two days a week. I was very comfortable and safe.

I have learnt that the steps of a righteous man or woman are ordered by God. He knows the way that we should take. He knows what challenges lie ahead. Soon after opening an immigration practice I faced my own challenges with the Home Office. My own immigration story was similar to many others before and after me. I initially came to the UK as a dependant of a student and then switched to a student visa. My husband then obtained a work permit. After completing five years on a work permit visa we applied for settlement. We tried to make a same-day application but the Home Office refused to accept our application. I did not even think much of it, thinking that since we had done nothing wrong we should just get our permanent residence.

In November 2007 my family received a shocking response from the Home Office. Our application had been refused. It had been refused with no right of appeal. The Home Office told us that since my husband had switched employers without changing his work permit we had been living illegally in the UK. We had valid leave to remain but the work permit was invalid as it was not linked to the school where he was currently working. I experienced so much fear, shame and anger at the response. I was scared about the future. We had made some investments in Zimbabwe but did not feel ready to go back. I had invested most of my money into our new business start-up. How could I practise as a solicitor with a problem with the authorities? What would I tell my children? I was embarrassed because I was already giving advice to people about their own immigration cases. I felt very angry with my husband for not checking with his school. I felt like a total fool for not checking with the Home Office myself.

I spent sleepless nights pondering what to do. I contacted a top lawyer in London and he advised me to return to Zimbabwe. I started looking at plans to migrate to Australia and started researching into all possibilities. After my tantrum-panic-fear-helpless cycle I decided to surrender this situation to God. I did not ask for prayer from anyone. I had to work this one out with God. God is so faithful. I realised that he knew what was ahead of me and had set people around me to encourage me so that I would be able to set up a law firm that would help me.

God answered me in a miraculous way. At that time I was not aware that there was a category for self-employed lawyers. I woke up at 4 am and somehow felt a leading to my computer. I googled "lawyers working for themselves with no visa". The search facility came up with the "Self-Employed Lawyers" category. I came across the visa category that I eventually applied for and was granted a new visa in less than four weeks. The process was so smooth; the caseworkers who dealt with this particular category were accessible by email and direct phone. I remember the caseworker joking with me and asking how I got into this predicament. He was so helpful and friendly.

I learnt to rely on God and to surrender all things to him. I believe God wanted to show himself as the Lord who provides, who directs and who leads. I also learnt to have compassion for the clients that I encountered along my journey. I had walked a mile in their shoes and therefore totally understood their anxiety, helplessness and pain that they encountered and faced.

In September 2013, after years and years in this country, we were finally granted settlement in the UK. Just to clarify – we always had a right to live in this country; it's just that it was not a permanent right. I recall seeing so many clients being granted settlement after having lived unlawfully in this country for years. I was happy for each one, cried with, and laughed with so many. I never felt, Oh why do I only have temporary leave to remain? I never actually thought about it but just celebrated with those who celebrated and cried with those who cried.

My work has always been a vocation. I have realised the limitations that are there from not having regular immigration status in the UK. I have seen the impact of migration on families and relationships, the stress caused by the uncertainty. I have seen that many people are affected by the move. In the Zimbabwean context most people came to the UK with the hope and belief that they would raise enough money to buy a house in Zimbabwe and then return home within 6 months. Some did not renew their immigration status. The migration from Zimbabwe to the UK caused so many social problems. People have suffered. Families have been broken apart, children have been affected in so many ways, and I have been privileged to share part of this journey with many people. Some left an indelible mark on my heart and I will never forget them. So many people profoundly impacted my life.

As an immigrant in this country I am proud to say that we have been able to set up our own law practice, purchase properties and educate our children. My husband and I have done this together; we have worked hard and not seen our immigration status or our race as a limitation. God has blessed us and we have been able to achieve some of our dreams and at the same time help many people who are in need of help.

We have now naturalised and are settled in England. I actually count myself to be blessed as I have two homes. Zimbabwe and England.

RETIREMENT

In general, when you hear about the word 'retirement' you always think of someone who has reached the time of leaving work due to old age and has to stop working. Before retirement there is a lot of preparation like saving some money, a secure place to stay, if children are still in education what's going to happen with their upkeep and on top of that the hidden anxieties of how one is going to spend their time and actually it's depression and anxiety together on how to spend your time.

It's really ridiculous as human beings we always want good things to happen to ourselves and we don't want even to think of bad things. We fail to understand that regardless of any faith we follow we are all created by God. I am not going into that because that's another subject on its own.

Retirement can come at any time, like what happened to me because of ill health. It came all of a sudden in November 2005. In my book *Through Pain to Popeye* I only explained a little about my work stoppage.

It happened all of a sudden when I was 53 years of age. I was working on night duty in charge of a nursing home for the elderly. All of a sudden I had no strength to even write a report to hand to the morning shift. I was taken in a wheelchair to a colleague's car and she dropped me at my doorstep thinking that it was just fatigue.

As I walked into my house I just plonked myself on the sofa and to be quite honest I can't remember what happened then. Winter had just started.

My thought was, I was going to be off sick for a couple of days and then go back to work. I couldn't stop thinking about going back to work because where I was working you were paid according to the hours you put in. For me the only thing I wanted to do was to clear all the debts which had accumulated since my husband had walked away on us leaving me facing all the financial mess.

It was a Friday evening when my daughter looked at me and I don't know what she saw; she asked if she should call an ambulance but I refused. She saw that I was not well and she phoned my nephew, who came in and in a loud voice stated, *'Auntie to the hospital, now!'* – to which I agreed.

I could see the gravity of my condition from all the examinations and observations done by the paramedics.

When I was lying on that hospital trolley before being admitted all I said was, *"Lord, I have come in here like a car in the garage for an overhaul, please do everything for me and I will work in Your Kingdom."*

I started seeing favour on me. Even the doctor asked me if I was related to my GP because I was sent for scans, x-rays and a lot of examinations and yet some patients have been waiting for a while to have all those done. (Devine connections.) Little did I know that that was the end of my nursing career after 33 years in the field of nursing.

Still retirement didn't sink in. Even my boss came visiting me at the hospital and asked me when I would be starting work again. I replied I didn't know. Work colleagues visited and expressed how they missed me at work.

I was in hospital for a month and I went through all tests, but still I wasn't strong enough to return to work.

My sick leave finished and I was then on statutory pay and, of course, I had nowhere to turn to except to take early retirement where you lose all pension scheme.

When I stopped working friends were few because no one wants to be associated with someone who's not well and not working. I couldn't even afford to pay for my registration. In all this I did have three friends who helped me, but I didn't tell them about my finances. As for my relatives, forget it, because now I was like a burden to them – but I thank God for my children.

From a nurse to a volunteer was a good journey for me because I have been able to use all my nursing knowledge and experience to help the people I met, and still meet, at those charities.

Early retirement has opened my mind. People who work long shifts don't have time to go even to a supermarket to buy healthy food, let alone big stores for clothes. Work is okay but have a "me" time where you buy even your favourite food or drink and say *"well done me"*; and above all thank God for all the strength and life, enabling you to work.

People work like borrowed secondhand bicycles: a borrowed secondhand bicycle is used hard to the point of no tyres because when the owner turns up for it, it will have done its job.

You begin to understand people more especially when you share the same sentiments. I call it a school of hard knocks where there is no teacher, no headmaster, but the homework you face has to be done in an orderly way.

I can budget well with the little money I get and this has taught me to take each day as it comes and relying solely on God, thanking Him for the air I breathe, sound mind and all the five senses working well. I call it *GRACE*.

Relatives and the outside world when they hear that you are retired already they think you are loaded with money and the outside world wants you to invest with them, but the bottom line is *they* don't know your story.

I have managed to have friends from where I volunteer and at church. Those who are still working the language has changed now and slowly I have cut my relationship with them. It took me a long time to live without extra cash as I used to have.

I found it very frustrating especially when people start talking about their jobs, especially at month end but I think I have come to terms with it now because the main thing is, I am alive, I am at peace, have become wiser and I still can bless others. That was after graduating from the school of hard knocks.

I have accepted what has come and gone in my walk of life and I still press forward because I know my tomorrow is better than today.

When you retire, or if retirement comes like a flood, as happened to me, stay tuned in faith and glorify your Provider who is God. Do not isolate yourself; try to be friendly and love your neighbours despite their religious beliefs. Know your neighbours by their names. There is a magic smile which shines if you are greeted by your name. Respect and love is the key as we live next door to people who don't even speak our language.

Retirement is not for the elderly only, it can bounce on you before you know. The main thing is, what do you do?

Push Mr Pride aside because retirement doesn't choose which colour, gender or class. I often give way to the elderly or disabled especially queueing for the bus because my motto is: '*We have to look after each other since we are the only ones who know what it is to be retired or getting on in life.*'

Next time you sit next to an elderly person just start a conversation; you will learn a lot on loneliness, maybe you are the first person they have spoken to that day.

A retirement bag brings a lot of wisdom, love, understanding and encouragement; to relatives it's portraying abuse of your finances if you are not careful because they ask what you want money for, and yet all these years you have worked hard supporting them so if you are not careful you will be told all the funerals to attend at your expense. Make sure you have a funeral policy so that your children won't face problems when you depart from this world. Write a will to avoid confusion because I have seen a lot of stupid things happening. Do not be afraid, you can always change your will if things go wrong.

My advice is put God first in what you do.

Choose wisely.

Don't give what you don't have.

Save money for the rainy day.

Go on holidays.

Enjoy your hobbies.

Spoil yourself once in a while.

Make genuine friends and pray with them.

Do not be taken away from your dream.

Learn to forgive at an earlier stage before it ruins you.

I am enjoying my retirement and I am useful to my family and the community. It was tough but I consider it a joy now because I put God first.

INVISIBLE CONDITION

Susan

Millions of people suffer from an invisible health condition and unless I've shared this with you, you'll be unaware that I suffer from Chronic Low Back Pain. This story shares details and emotions that I have never shared publicly before and I hope that this inspires anyone who thinks they may have been dealt a "raw hand" to drive themselves forward to success that I know is achievable.

At the age of 15, in November 1995, I was involved in a car accident. I was a front seat passenger in my mother's car when we hit a car in front at a low speed and then we were hit from behind by a jeep with bull bars. I initially had no pain, but we attended the A&E department anyway. By the time we were seen I had some neck, shoulder and low back pain. The doctor we saw wasn't concerned, no x-ray was taken, I was sent home to rest and take over-the-counter pain relief. Around a week later my neck and shoulder pain had eased but my back pain had worsened. My doctor prescribed some anti-inflammatory medication. For the next two months I visited my doctor on numerous occasions as what I'd been prescribed wasn't helping and more importantly the pain wasn't going away like I had been told it would.

In January 1996 I was finally referred for physiotherapy and was seen in January and February – this helped, but certainly didn't resolve the problem.

I would experience periods of low pain where it wouldn't bother me, to periods of intense pain where it would really impact on my mood and what activities I would be able to do. Imagine being a teenager and not being able to do everything your friends are doing. Sometimes I would carry on regardless, but then suffer big pain spikes and then emotionally this was a struggle.

The periods of intense pain came more frequently leading to more trips to see my doctor. I lost count of the different medical practitioners I saw, from my GP to Consultants, Pain Clinic Professionals, Reflexologists and Physiotherapists – it's a very long list. The list of treatments I had tried was even longer – nothing seemed to make any difference – some things eased the pain for a short time, but nothing enabled me to be pain free.

For a number of years I felt I wasn't taken seriously by medical professionals; they had seemed more concerned with my weight and why I was thin – this was my natural self! It was years before any proper investigation was carried out, all the efforts had been on "masking" the pain, rather than trying to resolve or understand the underlying cause.

Prior to the accident I had been a very active young lady, I loved taking part in sports like trampolining, running and swimming, however, since the accident my back pain worsened and as a result I stopped participating in sports. And as time went on I would actively avoid doing anything that might worsen my pain; even going out with friends was an extensive decision, rather than just "going with the flow" like you would expect any other teenager to do. By the time I was 19, I was largely inactive, my pain made worse when bending, lifting and standing/sitting for prolonged periods of time. This in turn impacted on my mood.

I hadn't realised at the time, but I really wasn't helping myself, I continued to wear high heels, go out dancing with friends at the weekends and tried to lead a normal life when in fact I was actually causing myself more issues in terms of the pain and hate cycle!

In 2004 after nine years of suffering, I was seen by an orthopaedic surgeon who took some side x-rays and found that at L5/S1 (lower spine) there was retrolisthesis which means that one of the vertebrae has moved out of alignment and my spine was very straight with a loss of the normal curve indicating spasms. This orthopaedic surgeon offered to operate in order to attach a system of screws, spacers and cord to realign and stabilise the spine – this is a high-risk procedure and therefore I decided on the basis I had full mobility and I was independent that I just couldn't take the risk. It was, however, a huge relief to finally have someone tell me *why* I was in so much pain. This explained why I would also experience discomfort and pain in my left shoulder and into my neck as spine posture affects the whole body.

From a career perspective I had a desire to become a paramedic. I had enrolled on a BTEC National Diploma in Health Studies at Northampton College to prepare for this. On starting this course I knew that the issues with my back would put me at a disadvantage to other candidates and unfortunately there wasn't a realisation until I was near to completing the course that I wouldn't be able to progress into my chosen field due to my injury.

Even considering all of the above, I have always been a really stubborn person (even from a very young age I'm told!). I was in paid work as soon as I was of age, which included: washing up in the local pub kitchen, waitressing, supervisor at KFC, supervisor at Little Chef – and yes, all of these jobs really did aggravate my pain, but what was the alternative? Sit at home and do nothing? It would have been too easy to have just stayed at home; my view was – and still is today – I would be no better staying at home.

Unfortunately, I had 10 days off sick in late 1998 at the request of my doctor and then a month off in 2005, only because I had reached a point where I was almost self-destructing – I am proud to say that this is the *only* time I have had off sick from work due to my back! Even during my month off I was making plans to help others until my best friend made me realise that I needed to help myself first.

I can't recall when from, but I was under the care of a Consultant Orthopaedic Surgeon in Oxford who was really positive and confident that he would be able to reduce my pain by an effective exercise programme, supported by pain relief. This may be unfair, but I felt from all the medical professionals I had previously seen he seemed to be the one that cared the most and appeared to be the most committed to helping me. I listened to what he said, I did what he said to do, and he was pragmatic with his approach which I liked. He got my pain relief to a place where it was being controlled most of the time – we settled on a Tramadol and Pregabalin combination; without the pain relief in place I could not have coped. I walked regularly, as well as doing Pilates and physiotherapy type exercises. However, I had some really big spikes of pain which was very emotional, and hard for those around me to really understand as it was all *invisible*.

I'm not someone who complains, but when I say my back is hurting, I mean I'm in extra pain beyond what I'm used to dealing with. The other reason that I don't usually mention it is that no one can do anything about it. I don't want, and have *never* wanted, sympathy.

My consultant retired and I was informed that I would have to go back through the junior members of the team which I was just not prepared emotionally to go back through, so I agreed with my GP that I wouldn't go back to Oxford on the basis I hadn't gained anything new from the appointments over the previous year and there had been no change to my condition.

In the years to come, I varied the exercises that I was doing (or not doing!) and by accident found that I wasn't experiencing the big spikes of pain that I had previously had when not doing my Pilates or physiotherapy exercises. I eventually stopped and felt better for it. I feel I have a responsibility here to say that this won't be the case for everyone and that each and every one of us is different, so don't copy me here please! In the end it was agreed by my doctor that the Pilates and exercises weren't helping and could possibly be giving me pain spikes. Over that period, I had also tried many new things at the gym, but had to stop because of increased back, neck and or shoulder pain.

Up until I was about 23 I felt like I was on a real emotional rollercoaster. You can imagine the types of feelings, *"why me?"*, *"it's not fair"* etc. I would make myself angry because of the situation I was in, I would be angry that I couldn't do all the things that my friends could do, and I decided that I would get some help with this and went to see a therapist in

Northampton who specialises in hypnotherapy and cognitive behavioural therapy. She really helped me to put all these feelings into perspective, gave me a whole raft of coping strategies, relaxation techniques and allowed me to deal with my condition in an effective way – and I continue today to draw on this.

This brings me on to archery, which really is the main part of this story, however, it's important for you to have a view of my past.

In 2011, a friend of mine had been to a country fair at which Northampton Archery Club had been running a stall, where you were able to have a go. The following weekend my friend was going to the club for an hour's taster session, and I didn't have anything on so decided to go with him.

We loved it, and booked onto a beginner's course. Each week couldn't come fast enough, and I completed my beginner's course in October 2011. For the 16 years following my car accident I can recall many scenarios where I've not been able to do something or having to give up on the things I loved doing, so finding archery was amazing for me.

I had initially started out shooting the recurve bow – which you may have seen in the Olympics. I instantly felt I had found my niche and very soon started competing at competitions (and winning!). I first shot for the Northamptonshire County Team in the summer of 2012; this made me feel amazing and hungry for more. In the summer of 2013 I had come second at a national level competition, beating GB archers and ranked 16th in the country that season.

Towards the end of 2013 and into 2014 I was experiencing many issues with my back, shoulders and neck. My neck had become particularly troublesome where some days any rotation would be really difficult, which was having a detrimental effect on my archery. A fellow archer helped me try and find a way to shoot. We changed my technique, hoping this would reduce the pain and suffering I was experiencing which had become really emotional as I thought this was the end of something else. I had reached the point where it was taking me numerous days to recover from shooting (which was meant to be enjoyable).

In May 2014, I was at a county match and not even halfway through the shoot when I had to retire because it hurt too much. I was in tears as I walked off the shooting line, knowing that I wouldn't ever shoot that bow again. Being someone who is *SO* stubborn, to admit defeat was emotional agony.

I had already discussed trying another type of bow with a fellow archer, which was the Compound bow (this is a much shorter bow, with a system of cables and pulleys). This bow works in a different way and means that at its peak draw (before releasing) the archer is holding less weight, usually 35-15% of the peak weight of the bow. This makes it much kinder to your body, particularly for those with health issues like mine.

I arranged to meet my friend to try a Compound bow, knowing that if I didn't like it that would be the end of archery for me, so I was feeling quite apprehensive. To be honest the bow scared me a bit, but I enjoyed it, and the following week I went and bought one. I had amazing help learning to shoot the Compound bow, but having shot the Recurve to a high standard, I didn't know if I could do the same, but as it turned out I should have switched over earlier and I really didn't have anything to be scared about.

At last... I was able to shoot more than one day in a row without experiencing any extra pain. That year (which was really half a season) I ranked 25th in the country, I achieved my GB outdoor qualification scores for the 2015 World Championships and was selected to represent England at the 2014 Senior National Indoors. I placed 8th at the National Indoor Championships 2014 and represented Great Britain at the 2015 European Indoor Championships.

However, in the summer of 2015, I woke to find that I couldn't move my neck, the muscles were heavily in spasm. It took me three hours to get out of bed, which was pretty scary. I couldn't recall doing anything to my neck or carrying out any activity that might have caused this. I was prescribed muscle relaxants and I wanted to explore whether the Pregabalin had caused the muscle spasms as this was a known possible side effect, so I immediately changed to another drug which unfortunately didn't ease the pain at all. I found myself in this horrible spiral of pain and no sleep cycle. Many days passed hoping for sleep as being awake was just too painful. I could only imagine what life could be like without any pain medication – no thank you!

The drug that I had been given was changed to Codeine, which I had taken previously for my back pain but had made me sleep my life away, but at least I knew it would give me the relief that I desperately needed. This was two weeks of my life that I don't ever want to repeat again. We eventually concluded later that year that the Pregabalin wasn't the cause as I had a further episode with my neck and therefore I reverted to this drug.

Throughout 2016 I had many success stories with my shooting, including being crowned British Indoor Champion 2016. And in 2017, I had my best outdoor season where I qualified and made the British team for the World Championships in Mexico, ranked 3rd in the Country and confirmed as a member of the 2018 GB National Squad.

This year I had the great honour of accepting two awards for both Northampton and Northampton-shire's *Local Sportswoman of the Year*. I also had the pleasure of switching on the town's Christmas Lights – who gets to do that?

For the past eight years I have worked for a market-ing agency in Milton Keynes. I manage some of our key clients as well as sitting on the company's Operating Board. I have other responsibilities too, which keeps me busy. Keeping busy helps me, even on the days where I am increasingly irritable, whether that's due to my pain or being exhausted from competing the weekend before!

I am extremely proud that I have had limited time off work, I have found something that I love to do in my spare time and worked hard to now own my own house. A typical week for me is working five days, training 4-5 times, some relaxation time and then little else! Relaxation time is really important to me and allows me to keep things in perspective in my life, and still today I use the tools that I learnt from my hypnotherapist.

There isn't a day that goes by where my shoulders aren't tight, where my back doesn't hurt, where I don't take tablets just to try and live a "normal" life that others have as standard. I say to people I meet that if you get the opportunity to try something new, do it. What have you got to lose? You may just find something that's life changing. Without archery, my life would be very different, and I don't think I would cope as well mentally with my health issues. Archery has given me something to focus on other than the pain! I'm proud to be standing next to and competing with other archers at an International level.

I am truly excited about what 2018 will bring and I really hope that my story inspires others to try new things, be more stubborn and to not give up. Because of my condition I have become an incredibly strong person; I don't give up without a very big fight, I love a challenge and I encourage other people to join me!

Always remember that the person next to you may have an invisible condition.

SOMETHING BRILLIANT

Polly-Ann

I have mental ill health. For this I am grateful as it may be what makes me brilliant.

The first diagnosis of my mental ill health came in my final year of university. I had a breakdown during this time and was diagnosed with depression and anxiety. I started taking medication, and had my first period of counselling. At the time, it was thought to be a short-term illness driven purely by the stress of my final year. This was 20 years ago. I have now discovered that depression, anxiety, medication and counselling is my 'normal'. And I'm OK with that.

Since then, I have avoided going back to Bristol where I studied for my degree. In fact, I have only returned once since my final exam, and that was for my graduation. I have attempted to visit since, but found it too difficult, too claustrophobic and too emotional, and promptly turned round on the M32 and fled.

Last summer, I went back. It was a chance visit where the intention wasn't to visit Bristol, but circumstances meant it came about. I then found myself near the house I had lived in. The house the breakdown had happened in, where my whole world changed, and my future trajectory became something else.

What struck me on the walk up the street was how the house was opposite an amazing park. A beautiful open park but with enough trees to create a small oasis in a city. Why had I never been to the park when I lived there? It was literally over the road. I stood on the street and looked at the building, with a fabulous park behind me.

As I left Bristol, I reflected. Why did I never go to the park? Why did I not visit places and see the culture? Why did I never sit in a coffee shop and watch the world go by? I saw more of Bristol in that recent weekend than I ever had while I was studying there.

Of course, the answer is clear now. I didn't have the tools to know how to look after myself emotionally. I could do all the practical things of course, and I knew my objective, my sole objective: get your degree. Work. Work. Work. You are nothing without this degree. Keep working. And so, I did.

Yet, one simple thing could have changed what happened. I could have gone to the park. I could have put down the pen and sat in the park. I could have felt the fresh air and seen the trees. I could have stopped and drunk the coffee. I could have been in the moment for five minutes. I didn't know that then.

As it happens, I am grateful for what happened. Of course I am because it was the start of me knowing how to take care of my mental wellbeing. But now, I want to scream from the rooftops to all students:

"YOU ARE SO MUCH MORE THAN YOUR DEGREE. GO OUTSIDE AND SIT IN THE PARK. DRINK THE COFFEE. FEEL THE AIR. BREATHE. YOU ARE BRILLIANT."

Now, 20 years on, I have the mind space to be able to reflect back. I can recognize that year was all part of me becoming who I am. Just another chapter of my journey. I can now see that what happened in my final year of university was not the beginning of my mental ill health. It had been there for much longer. Unrecognised and confused, causing internal conflict because I didn't know what to do with the feelings. The feelings that was causing an imbalance between what I felt was expected of me, and what I felt was authentic for me.

All these years later, surprisingly to me, I now know my mental ill health makes me brilliant. Who would have thought that the single most challenging thing of my life turned out to be a gift? Of course, this could just be my narrative to ensure I am 'OK' with the journey my life has taken. Now I have learnt how to utilise the tools I have acquired, I can say this. I couldn't say this 20 years ago. I wouldn't have dared to.

By no means am I taking away the severity and impact mental ill health can have. It can destroy people and relationships. It can challenge every aspect of your life. It can cause pain and hurt on an hourly basis. It can control decisions and impact the smallest aspects of your being. For some people, as we all know too well, it can be too much. The whirlwind of negative emotions are all too familiar to me.

If I was in the midst of an episode at the moment, I would be questioning my own thoughts to even be contemplating that I am grateful for my depression. But, what if it was the most impactful thing in my life, and without it I would be 'normal'. And, normal would be alright of course. Normal was achieving and being, but for me, would I be feeling or being authentic?

I look back, and every crucial time period of my life, every key decision, every step on my journey has come from my depression. The heightened impact it has on my thinking. The processing of how to become a better person and how to overcome barriers. The thinking. The reflecting. The constant working on my own mental wellbeing. The knowing that I am on the edge, and one small whisper of wind can knock me over that edge. So I ask myself, why don't I live there? Why do I try and be miles from the edge where it is supposed to be safe and comfortable, because what if it's not my version of safe and comfortable once I got there anyway? Why not embrace the place my depression takes me to? From a period of depression, I make good, sound, decisions based on sense and wellbeing. To others, they will seem illogical and perhaps manic decisions, but that's because they are not in the safe place I create teetering on the edge. I work so hard at sense checking my decisions, processing, thinking, thinking, thinking ... that they could never be anything but good decisions. I reflect on facts and not emotions. However, I hold true, we have one life and one opportunity to be the best we can be, so I take what some see as risks.

How has this affected my working career? Well, this is the interesting thing.

Let's go back. This is challenging because how far back do you go when something is so fundamentally wrapped up in who you are and not just the career path you took? But let's go back to university age. I wanted to do psychology at university. I can't recall the decision process, but I actually did a business studies degree. Maybe, it was because I could see a clear career path from that. There was clear direction and a process I could follow. At the time, I felt comfortable with direction and process; predictability. I got 'the' placement year that everyone wanted at Hewlett Packard. I got on a treadmill of corporate commercialism. I went on to work in recruitment, and then to work for Mars on 'the' training scheme that everyone was trying to get on. I didn't stop to think if it was what I wanted as I was on that bus, and it was already going. I was driven, determined and successful. And so, the bus journey continued. And, I was ticking boxes – financial security, status, success. I have worked for some of the largest food brands in the UK as well as the largest own-label brands. I've worked with familiar customers worth millions, and I've made decisions that impact people and businesses.

I started to think about what had made me successful in my career. It was the relationships I held with my customers and the people that worked with me. It was the way I interpreted the situation, the information, and from it delivered a clear message. It was the ability to reflect, stand back from a situation and gain clarity that I could then empower my team to have this same clarity. It was the dynamic character I brought to the table.

At the same time, I realised that some of the parts of myself that I had hidden from many people for so many years were the foundations of what makes me brilliant. I was never open about my mental ill health at work. I even went so far as to lie on pre-medical questionnaires, or use the word 'mild' or 'brief period of' before the words depression and anxiety as if that made it OK. I can confirm there is at times nothing mild about my depression and anxiety, and it has not been for a brief period! No one questioned it, so I never expanded on it. I saw it as a weakness. I feared that if people at work knew, they would think I was not capable or maybe that I was 'flaky'. Every doctor's appointment or counselling session I had was out of work hours. I was determined no one at work would have the opportunity to believe I was less than able.

I undertook a career-coaching pathway myself to ensure I would make the right decision for my future. One of the most valuable exercises I did was identifying my values. Integrity was key. Balance, worth, energy, authenticity, compassion. More interesting were the values I did not want in my career ... status, fame, affluence. Everything I had achieved in my career so far, summed up values I didn't actually identify with. I questioned myself, was I demonstrating the values I did identify with in my career? Was I showing integrity? How could I be me?

Some said my next step was brave, I just felt it essential. I left the food industry in January 2017.

I no longer hide my mental ill health because I feel the tools, techniques and the way I manage this gives me the ability to see beyond and gain clarity. Better still, what if I could help other people realise that mental ill health was not a barrier to success?

Since leaving the security of the corporate world and setting up my own business, I have really reflected about why would the tools and techniques that help me cope with mental ill health be of use in the business world. When I think about leadership and the qualities required to be a strong leader, two stand out for me: trust and empathy. Without these two things, we cannot take people on a journey with us or indeed be on their journey. We build trust and empathy by believing in someone else's reality and by accepting their viewpoint, regardless of whether we agree with or understand that viewpoint.

'*Before you criticise a man, walk a mile in his shoes.*' We've all heard this phrase, most famous for being adapted from Harper Lee's *To Kill a Mockingbird*:

> *"You never really understand a person until you consider things from his point of view, until you climb into his skin and walk around in it."*

This greater empathy and ability to build trust from having experienced mental ill health comes from knowing that there are many shades of grey in our lives. There is no black and white, but a shade of grey that you feel comfortable with which may of course change as you grow and develop along your journey. It comes from knowing the dark and being able to appreciate the light. I can reflect on my own journey and appreciate that my reality changes as my movement from dark to light changes. Key here is being able to see someone else's reality, and how it may change. From this empathy we build the trust to enable us to lead our colleagues and customers successfully.

However, how often do we do this in our roles? In our roles as leaders, parents, teachers and friends, how often do we put ourselves in the shoes of our colleagues or our friends and try and feel their story? Not just listen to it but feel it? Do we make it real? Do we embrace the dialogue and narrative? Do we enter into it with an open mind? If we can appreciate their viewpoint we can understand it. We can work with that. We can build from that. We can understand their need because a need requires a solution. Whether this is a negotiation for a vast amount of commercial business, or equally whether this is a colleague confiding in you, listen and understand the other person's viewpoint. Build empathy for their reality and reasoning, and therewith comes trust.

To contradict myself completely here would be to say that when in a discussion with someone who may suffer from mental ill health, I would advise that you don't try and understand their reality. Accept it, but also accept you may never understand it. If you have never experienced mental ill health, then understanding it will be very challenging. In fact it may even sound absurd when they try and explain their reality to you. In this instance you don't need to understand. You just need to accept and show empathy. From this comes trust that they are not alone on their journey. Equally you will not be able to solve it for them. We are programmed to be so solution focused, but think small next step actions here and not about solving the problem.

Leadership is about trust and empathy. Power from belief. Strength on a journey from believing in someone else's real life. I feel from the coping mechanisms I put in place to help me 'function' in the corporate world, I developed an ability to have empathy with others which aided my career. Was I the best sales person? Not at all, far from it. But, I had fabulous relationships with my customers which meant they remained loyal to my organisations as long as commercially viable. I was able to mentor my team to enable them to be the best they could be. I was always keen to gain clarity, and those who worked with me would be humoured by my love of a flip chart to gain that clarity. Part of that was me being able to rationalise the thought process for myself, so I would draw it or write it down, and take everyone else with me on that journey. Primarily, it was my coping mechanism.

I am aware I make this sound like an easy path to have been on. Obviously, that isn't the case. There have been times in employment when multiple triggers for my mental ill health have come along all at once and I have struggled to cope with those challenges. Sometimes, I haven't coped well at all. The ironic thing is, the biggest trigger has always been that I am failing and not making a success, as I perceived it at the time, of myself. Which has then spiralled into me consequently not coping and not being the best version of me.

For me, most of this 'failing', as I perceived it, would happen when I wasn't at work. I would put all my energy into coping and delivering, and being 'successful' at work, which meant by the time I got home, sadly there wasn't always the energy to then be able to do the same at home. I'm very aware now, I had that division of energy imbalanced. What can I say, we are all work in progress. One of my coping mechanisms (which I now recognise was not always helpful) was that as things in work became more out of my control, I inflicted greater control into other areas of my life. More routine, more structure, more rhythm and order. I felt it helped me stay on track, and in the midst of experiencing the dark times, it may well have done. I have learnt to embrace the lack of order that is sometimes refreshing in my life now. As I write this, I am still aware that my version of 'lack of order' is vastly different from others. But, it's my version, and it works for me.

So, all this reflection and awareness I now have, what would it have been like if I had realised this at the time my breakdown or through my early career years? How would it look if some of the workplace 'rules' were taken away, so we could all be more successful? What would it have been like if we recognised what worked well from our personalities regardless of how that skill or technique got there? What if we had made empathy an acceptable and encouraged skill? What would it have been like if my fear of failing had been realised as that which was actually driving me to be successful?

It would feel like my life now. Being honest and authentic in my work and home. Recognising that my mental ill health, the mechanisms I use to cope, the empathy I have developed are actually the foundations of me and who I am. It's what has made me brilliant. And, I am grateful for that.

JOHNNY'S HAPPY PLACE

Denise

Johnny was born on September 18ᵗʰ, 1985 and died on Thursday, October 23ʳᵈ, 2014.

A short life but one he had enjoyed immensely. From the time he could talk he had fun. He found life fun and amazing. He was wise beyond his years. He understood things that others didn't. From an early age he knew how to talk to people about anything and that brought him many friends and a wonderful reputation. Yes, he could be downright stupid but he also knew how to help others. He somehow knew about injustices before it had ever been explained to him. It was natural for him to sit and talk to people about their problems and to try to encourage them to take the right path in life. He was so charismatic. A great deal of charm that was always very natural. He was never fake. His kindness to others was heart-felt always. Like a lot of people who are going through difficulties, he was always able to direct others into a good place but never for himself. He always knew the direction he should be heading for but it was always the other direction he took. He became a very convincing liar. Anyone who has had a loved one hooked on drink and drugs will recognise that all too clearly. I desperately needed to know his whereabouts but I very rarely heard about the real location, like one time he was late home for dinner. I'd tried contacting him throughout the day. Eventually he answered, told me that he was in Market Harborough and would be home by 6pm. Six o'clock came and went, all through the night I phoned until eventually I got hold of him at 5 the next morning and he was in London. He'd never been to Market Harborough the previous day; he'd been walking the streets of London all night. He was sitting in a café when eventually I got through to him. I pleaded with him to come back and he did later that night. This was the week he died.

What a dreadful few days we had. I will spend the rest of my life wondering about all the "what if's" and "if only". It makes my suffering all the more acute but I can't prevent myself from doing it. How could I, his mother, have possibly averted this most dreadful of outcomes. Which path should I have taken? He was so adorable. I loved living with him. We were so in-tune with each other. We never rowed but we did know how to talk and laugh. Life with Johnny was always so interesting. He really did have a lot to live for but to take drugs you need money; if you don't have money but you still take drugs you end up owing your dealer. I had no choice at this point but to pay the dealer myself. He would come to me terrified saying that he has to pay over the money NOW. At the end of his life I didn't know how much he owed or whether or not the dealers were after him. I think he feared for my safety. People knew where he lived and if he didn't pay up he, I think, was worried that harm would come to me. "If I die now your grief will be short lived, if I carry on living your grief will go on forever". Of course I told him that this was so very wrong. He knew desperately I loved him; he knew that there was a strong possibility that if he died I would shortly follow. I too believed this to be true. I knew I couldn't live without him, the thought was totally unbearable but because our rock solid love I had convinced myself that he would never commit suicide. He might run away but he could never take his own life. How very wrong I was. God, how naïve, how stupid, how ridiculously over confident was I to believe that his overwhelming problems could be outweighed by even something as strong as our love.

There are a myriad of stories I could recount about Johnny's life. The incredibly good deeds he did which I didn't become aware of until after his death. The happiness he brought to others, the endless stories of how he would improve the dullest of situations. He was such an impressive young man who sort of glided through life when things were going well. He spent a few years in Yorkshire but whenever he came home, which was very regularly, he couldn't wait to park up his van and saunter through the streets of Kettering. He knew hundreds of people and walking through the town with him would take such a long time because every few moments we would stop and talk to a whole stream of people. But of course there was the very dark side. The side that would have me pacing the kitchen floor throughout many nights. I daren't leave the house in case he'd phone because he ran away so many times: Scotland, France, Devon, and Bristol. Once he cycled up the entire east coast of England. He could be so unpredictable. Even though he was "clean" when he died, drugs killed him. My daughter Charlotte and I both believe that his suicide was an act of selfless bravery. He *DID* die to save us. He *WAS* a martyr.

Before his death he had written a most glorious book which he entitled *Norman the Caterpillar*. Charlotte knew that this has to be published because it was totally glorious. She worked so hard for the next six months to piece together this beautiful piece of work. She collaborated with the illustrator Steff Lee, to get the characters to look exactly as she wanted them and she did the most exquisite job. Charlotte brought all the characters together in a unique and very exciting way. She brought them to life in an extraordinary manner. She has never done anything like this before. Hours and hours of work lay ahead of her when she took on this project and her fabulous work paid off. Nothing short of genius. She too, like Johnny, is quite a remarkable lady. No one could have done more or tried harder to save Johnny. She knew all the warming signs and spent many, many nights crying and worrying about it, trying to find suitable places where he could get the help he needed. Even though he himself knew he needed to get psychiatric help he always seemed to shun it. "Only I can get rid of my demons" is what he would say.

I used to fear death. I am approaching my 70th birthday but I never thought I'd ever reach it. My mother died aged 58 and my father 60. I cannot believe this milestone is just around the corner but if I died tomorrow I would die in the belief that Johnny and I would be reunited. I have to convince myself of this otherwise I would go mad. We will float around the heavens as we promised each other many, many years ago. We would explore the black holes, hand in hand we will drift along the Milky Way. It will happen so no, I don't fear death anymore, instead it will be the most exciting adventure ever and one day, in 60 years or so, my beloved daughter will join us on this epic voyage, together, all of us, the way it should be.

We started a café called *Johnny's Happy Place*. We kicked off by holding a Christmas craft fair in December 2014, two months after Johnny died. I would never have believed that I could do it. There was no way that I would have the strength to keep talking about

Johnny all day but I did. Hard, but I knew that I had to do it and the room was full of buyers and sellers – all there because of Johnny – *my* Johnny. Of course I would find the strength.

Once we established a venue we got started. We operate from a building that was bequeathed to the youth of Kettering. The building is a charity in itself and run by a committee who oversee all that goes on at *Keystone*. We were offered a room there, in desperate need of a makeover, to operate out of every weekend. A week or so before we got our hands on our room at Keystone we were invited on BBC Radio Northampton to talk about our plan and ideas. Following our radio interview we were contacted by lots of wonderful people wanting to offer their services. To them we are indebted. Along with family and friends, old and just made, we got rid of all the brightly coloured walls in favour of a more neutral and calming white; we set to in getting furniture from various charity shops. Johnny loved Jackson Pollock so the majority of chairs and tables are a covered in splashy paint in the Pollock style. We have a bike on the wall to symbolise Johnny's love of cycling and his infamous ability to balance bikes on his chin (as well as bird tables, school tables, ladders – anything really!). It's a lovely place. I relish being there every Saturday and Sunday. We offer warmth and love and a huge amount of caring to all who walk through our doors.

Our aim was to encourage those with any sort of mental health issue such as loneliness or anxiety to enter our café and feel welcomed and not judged. We offer "pay what you can" food and drink and don't turn anyone away. We are open to everyone: young, old, rich and poor, good mental health, and bad mental health. We do get quite a few homeless and rough sleepers; anyone who can't afford a meal gets a free main course and pudding in addition to as much tea and coffee as they want. Johnny was homeless for a while when he was in Bristol. He was helped enormously by St Mungo's, a very worthwhile charity which covers a huge area. They fed and clothed him, helped him find a place to live and a job. Within ten days of Johnny's death we raised over £4000 for them.

The café is a place of joy safety and they are always thanking us for creating this happy place where they can bring their children, do craft work organised by our wonderful volunteers, some of whom have had a lifetime of trauma due to what has happened to them or their own children. We love them all and are so very grateful for all their hard work and the enormous effort they put in to running JHP every weekend. I would personally like to thank all of our guests who frequent our café on a regular basis. They are such a cross section of people, but without them I don't know how I would have coped over the past three years. It has given me a purpose, a purpose that Johnny would have wholeheartedly embraced. He, with every fibre of his body, loved and helped so many and it is my job now to continue his legacy. He was so extraordinary and talented and I miss and love him every minute of every day but the café has permitted me to show others the love that Johnny would have showered on them all.

I have to thank all of my family for the enormous help they gave me during Johnny's life. The wise words, the physical effort in order to create a life that Johnny's would want to live in. Nothing we did could ever have prevented him from going on October 23rd, to end his own life.

We all adored him and will continue to do so until our own lives come to an end.

Thank you darling Johnny. All of these people, the majority of which didn't know you, now feel as though they did know you. Even in death you are helping a whole new group of lovely people.

~

We are open every Saturday 10-4 and Sunday 11-2.

We operate by donations only – a "pay what you can" operation.